EPICS 2: Spy Included

S. E. McKenzie

ISBN-13: 978-1-928069-72-0
ISBN-10: 192806972X

DEDICATION

To everyone who has been left out in the cold

THIS BOOK IS A BOOK OF SPECULATIVE FICTION. Characters, companies, governments, places, events, are either products of the author's imagination or used fictitiously. Any resemblance to persons (living or dead), companies, governments, places and/or events, is a coincidence.

CONTENTS

STARE

#15. THE STARE

I

You knew it wasn't fair
Wherever you went
They had to stare.

As if you weren't really there.

The Stare was everywhere;
The glare of hate and the toxic state
Was the pull of Monopolistic Power

To make it his own
He excluded others all around
Even those who shared his ground;

How did legislating poverty oppress?

Victim of process
Had no access
Or no address

And Monopolistic Man; a shell of a man;
Didn't care;
He traded his water and air

For cold cash which just got devalued.

His snobocracy
Was the new aristocracy
Hidden behind words of an old meritocracy.

His Monopolistic Style flared his stare
While his rage grew
Between his eyes.

His glare needed no disguise
It pierced through your personal space,
His stare surrounded your face

As if you weren't there.

Marginalized and excluded;
Many said they cared
About their water and air

Beware of the Fallen Angel

Under his spell of hypocrisy
His self-fulfilling prophecy
Can come true

EPICS 2: Spy Included

How did legislating poverty oppress?

Victim of process
Had no access
Or no address.

Under reconstruction
With barriers and obstruction
Never questioned the lies and his corruption

For this man so monopolistic
Was naturally simplistic
At times even sadistic

As he traded the water and air
For cold cash
Which just got devalued.

He demanded
Monopolistic Control
Without disguise

Even though
A Pluralistic Goal
Was far more a Natural Role.

There was no compromise

For Internal Controls
Change on demand
Not on command;

External Controls
Guns and bombs
No faith in love;

As monopolistic man's rage grew
He demanded one way control
Never remembering a name

Because as he stared
Everyone looked the same
In his very own sum-zero game

There was always someone to blame
For the winner; life would never be the same
As Monopolistic Man grew into the dominant role.

His child dreamed
His wife screamed
For Monopolistic Man had his foot in the door

He said, "this is the only social order that is right
One way; one fight
My way every night

Or take the only highway in sight.
If you won't show deference to me
It is your loss, I am the boss

I don't want you here no more;

I will close every single door;
Surrounding you
Never to open the way doors did before."

And Monopolistic Man said,
"There is no goal greater than mine
For my One-Way-World suits me fine."

And they all held on to the key
Their way to fight
Against their own poverty.

The power to share was the multiplier
Though Monopolistic Man; a shell of a man;
Called Truth a liar

Love watched as many died.
Love was ignored but could still inspire
As the solution was burning in Truth's fire

Love had a pulse and a heart
Love watched the overkill
Of the underfed and cried

Monopolistic Man
Journeys through life
Possessing what he can

Monopolistic Man; a shell of a man;
Becomes a killing machine
When needing a way to fulfill his dream

While his child dreamed
His wife screamed
Monopolistic Man had his foot in the door

Hell's Hate closed the gate
During this monopolistic fate
More than just another State of Hate.

EPICS 2: Spy Included

Affordable pads were called slums
The tenants were all called bums
Love was an equalizer; you know it was true,

But Monopolistic Man; a shell of a man;
Needed a slave
Just like you.

How could you know
What your future had in store
When Monopolistic Man demanded so much more?

There was a path
That you were not allowed on
For it was behind the gate which controlled fate.

To take the path was the goal of some.
While Monopolistic Man; a shell of a man;
Called this act trespass against his class.

For the gate to equal opportunity
Was closed; buried under clause after clause
And Monopolistic Man said,

"Follow the One-Way-Rule
For going the wrong way
Makes you a fool."

Monopolistic Man ruled by his might.
Every wrong; he called right;
He threw us fire when he promised light;

Self-fulfilling prophecy
Needed no light to see
For his Way was the only way

For Pluralistic Goals just got in the way
And they were too complicated
Anyway

It was so easy
To do one task one way
Every day;

To own the means
And to satisfy physical needs
One must own the control lines

EPICS 2: Spy Included

How did legislating poverty oppress?

Victim of process
Had no access
Or no address.

For the paver of every new path
Needed a light to shine
In order to grow during the night.

You will be born alone and die alone.
Best to have a heart of stone
For Monopolistic Man

Says he is the only one who can
Unseal fate
To free you to be who you can be.

For Monopolistic Man
Owned Power and Might
While fake light shone during the night

Easing Paralyzing Fright

Even though Fear was the tool
Of Monopolistic Man; a shell of a man;
Giving more might to a fool.

Love could change his ways
For Love was allowed to define you
Until the end of your days

Under this ever changing sky.

II

You were so classified
They lied as you cried
While the cause of your pain was denied

A nickname was given
To symbolize
Your place so social

The stare glared out their hate,
To justify their rule so cultural,
Love was delayed, and arrived too late.

EPICS 2: Spy Included

Without love
It was so easy
To discriminate

For how could they know how to tolerate?

Victim of process
Had no access
Or no address.

They were so dehumanized
They criticized his tone
As they laughed

He was all alone.

The watchers were organized
Fallen angels from above
Easier for them to hate than to love

So polarized
In misunderstanding
Lost communication channels

Hate grew from different angles
Euphemisms were said
As a heart was stolen

And resold
For gold
And treasure

Filling their lives with pleasure
A new future was in the air
The mass did not know how to prepare

In a polarized world with so little care
Polarization was never fair
And to fight for love made heroes of some

How did legislating poverty oppress?

Victim of process
Had no access
Or no address.

Though many would trade
Their water and air
For cold cash which just got devalued;

While others waited for the sun
To shine again
After the rain

EPICS 2: Spy Included

The air smelled so sweet.
While the ones on their list
Were watched day after day

Made future persecutions more neat.

Dumped in a desert
Without food for mind nor heart
The vulture culture

Tore many apart;
Said to be no longer human
For they had lost their heart.

And Traded
Their water and air
For cold cash which just got devalued;

Victim of process
Had no access
Or no address.

And in the sky
There was a toxic cloud
Talking about it was not allowed

Warm air rose into the cold
Violent gusts of wind
Moved the toxic cloud

Over our heads;
Monopolistic Man; a shell of a man;
Still takes what he can

Exterminated
Those he hated
While the tears dropped gently from the sky.

How did legislating poverty oppress?

Victim of process
Had no access
Or no address.

So demoralized;
Could not walk or talk nor cry,
The pain was so subjective

And some stood apart
And saved
Their heart.

And some were too
Willing to believe the lie
So they did not have to cry.

III

Monopolistic Man had his glossy magazine;
If you didn't look like a super model
He would treat you real mean.

Your pain was your chain;
They said Divine Love
Came from above;

You knew that real love
Could only come
From a pure heart;

So dehumanized
Was Monopolistic Man
His fat stomach got in the way

As he ran;

Toward a promise
That was already broken
And he too had pain which had awoken.

The promise was misleading;
It promised love
Without any feeling;

And now Monopolistic man
Was close to ruin;
What was unfair could not be proven;

For the ruiner
Did not care what was at stake
And gave very few an even break.

Monopolistic Man could not help but stare;
There was so much suspicion in the air.
Monopolistic Man; a shell of a man;

Hoped that something was wrong

For he had far less than you;
While his jealousy grew
Into malice and false pride.

Monopolistic Man
Hoped for something to control
Then his stare fell upon you;

EPICS 2: Spy Included

He traded
His water and air
For cold cash which just got devalued

Made him madder
As the green devil
Took over his head;

Monopolistic Man; a shell of a man;
Wished that you were dead.
He did everything he could to humiliate

He was a slave to Hate

Which paved his fate.
When his energy ran out
It was then too late.

How did legislating poverty oppress?

Victim of process
Had no access
Or no address.

THE END

HIDDEN

#16. HIDDEN

I

Standing above
Without love
Subjectively

Selfishly
Hypocritically
Eyes refusing to see

The more they persecuted
The more they feared
The persecuted

During the denigration
No hope for negotiation
No concern for humanization

It is said there is a back door
For
Image I Nation

Hard to find
When one is blinded
By degradation

A hurt sensation
For the last Generation
Without a title

The more they persecuted
The more they feared
The persecuted

Hold on for the Push
Stand tall for the Pull
Consume until full

By those hidden behind blank eyes so dull
As they push and shove
To get ahead in their culture without love

To speak out was never enough
Unreasonable, Unsustainable
Behind a wall, so much is unattainable

The more they persecuted
The more they feared
The persecuted

EPICS 2: Spy Included

Their side of the street
Was behind a wall of concrete
Where they had never enough to eat

Where life moved to the speed of a crawl

Treated like bugs
Undeserving of hugs
Labelled as slugs

The more they persecuted
The more they feared
The persecuted

People crossed the street
Refused to integrate
Felt too much hate

Called the persecuted thugs
Fear was now mixed with hate
Lack of co-operation controlled fate

Successful denigration
Look away
Don't try negotiation

Do as the label implies
Do not hear their painful cries
For now they have been ghettoized.

The more they persecuted
The more they feared
The persecuted

Behind the wall
So unethical
Still looking for the back door

May be just mythical
Truly unsustainable
Ghettoized

When they were young and able

II

Manipulation
Dehumanization
Forbidden and hidden

EPICS 2: Spy Included

Distain
Complain
Detain

So denigrated
Trapped in a force of hatred
Nothing was negotiated.

The more they persecuted
The more they feared
The persecuted

For they are now all behind the wall.
Looking for a back door
So they can escape what has happened before

Wood-chipper diplomacy
No evidence based democracy
Seen by eyes closed in prayer

Eyes that would not see
As if the victims
Were not there

Paralyzed by bureaucracy;

Totalitarian control
No longer able
To change their role

No longer believing
In the power
Of Soul

Push and shove
Culture without love
Believed cruelty was justified

The more they persecuted
The more they feared
The persecuted

Prayed for a greater might
Left the homeless
Destitute in middle of the night

Bulldozed whatever they could
To create their super-highway
Of push and shove

A world without love

EPICS 2: Spy Included

The legacy
Of totalitarian control
No more time for a leisurely stroll

The more they persecuted
The more they feared
The persecuted

This was Wood-Chipper Diplomacy
Cutting down every tree
Which might be blocking a view or two

So denigrated
It was hard to not
Return the hatred

Just another trap
On the dead-end
Road to hell

Denigration
Force destroying one's value
Defamation

So dictated
Made some sadistic
Others valued this power of hatred

The more they persecuted
The more they feared
The persecuted

So attached to the food chain politic

The more they persecuted
The more they feared
The persecuted

Could turn it all around
As technology helped the damaged
Take back their ground

Persecution so cruel
Mistreatment meant to drive away
Rivals and competition

Now the process
Could be turned around
The persecutors said

Feeding the persecuted was said to be wrong
For the persecuted would grow too strong
Could turn the process all around.

The cause for Malice was hidden
Entry into the wrong-way zone
Was forbidden

The more they persecuted
The more they feared
The persecuted

As the flood waters moved in
Black Bird from afar
Made her nest

In the hole in the wall.
And sang a song
As the promise of a new world

Moved along time
That never stood still
For that was the way of the Will.

THE END

BLUE

#17. BLUE

I

Blue was just a girl
Who lived in a town
That was sometimes sunny and bright.

There was a rule of order
And hierarchy
Deciding what was wrong and right.

There was a great love of things
All around
While the homeless slept hidden

Outside on the ground.
The atmosphere so thin
Was blue too

During a dark and rainy night
Common Sense was found hanging in a tree.
The shock and sadness

Overwhelmed this little society.
All the great powers to be
Had nothing much to say

For Common Sense
Depended on trust
Without fear

To grow
Into tomorrow
Without shedding a tear.

And the places where Common Sense had been
Though few and far between
Caused Fear Culture to dread

Words that instigated
Hatred
For Common Sense.

Others said
Common Sense was part of a plot
To take control

Over the External Force's role.
Which was why
Common Sense was shot.

EPICS 2: Spy Included

The Authorities
Disclaimed
Such a claim.

Some did admit that Common Sense
And the Downtrodden
Had been forgotten

Which was rotten

Common Sense, Just like True Love
When denied; may have died;
From a broken heart.

Needed a fresh start

True Love knew
That she was the answer too
True Love knew

The girl called Blue
Knew too
That true love

Gave so much to live for.
They say that Common Sense
Always knew too.

As the days went by
The tune had changed
A story had been arranged.

Some said Common Sense had to die
Even though sadness filled the air
More rumors began to spread

Many were glad and said
The death of Common Sense
Was justified

And called it suicide
Said it was rumored
That Common Sense had died

Through its own hand

Many said they saw Common Sense
Walking down the street
With rope; could not cope.

Such a story was hard to believe
That Common Sense
Would die in such a way

For Common Sense did not let emotions rule;
Or allow False Love
To make it look like a fool.

"All over town
So many were kicked down
For their own good," Fear Culture said

"Must be done while still young."

"One's fitness to live free
Must be questioned
By every Authority,"

Legalist said.

II

The tone was hard
Though never thought to be cruel
For order was the rule

Some said False Pride
Of the well to do
Made a target out of Blue too.

Others said it was the economical
Thing to do
And never a plot defined

To demolish Blue's mind.

So frozen in fear
Blue
Could no longer dream.

Wherever she went
People would scream
In her ear

Leaving Echoes to fear
Dwelling in her head
True Love shed a tear

Outside on the ground.
The atmosphere so thin
Was blue too

During another cold dreary night
True Love came to Blue's bed
And said,

"Blue, I am here for you,
Give good folks
Another try

Common Sense
And Dispositional Attribution
Will one day join again

One day there will be
A better place
Where we will both want to live,"

True Love
Said
"I hope I never die."

And Blue said,
"I do too."
True Love proclaimed,

"There will be a better place
Of my design
Where my name will never be forgotten

For where there is True Love
Every face
Will be cherished

Where there is no more sorrow
Or abuse of power
Where we will be allowed the time to smell a flower

Without being accused
Nor being abused
Or used."

III

As the years went by
Blue no longer knew how to dream
As fear culture made remembrance

Of the day Common Sense
Was found
Hanging in the tree

Common sense so forgotten
Awoke in pain
To rule again.

THE END

GREEN

#18. GREEN

I

Green
Was living his third stage of life
As a happy frog

He often sat on a log
Near the bog
Watching the flies go by.

As a tadpole
He enjoyed living almost like a fish,
But those days are gone.

His log
Gave him a path
To leave the water.

Once his legs had grown;
It was said
That he was a handsome frog

Sitting on a log
Watching the flies
Go by.

II

Green was sitting on his log under the sun
Wondering if this new day
Would be fun.

And there was Boy
Who was watching Green
For Green was the prettiest frog

Boy had ever seen.
And Boy wanted to keep
Green for a pet.

Boy did not understand
That his jar in hand
Would be repressive

Regressive
And could lead to death
For Green.

Boy was not mean;
Boy did not understand
The power of the Tight-Lid-Jar in his hand

For Tight-Lid-Jar Society
Closed in on some
So a tune was not free and could not come.

And Green's world revolved around the sun;
While a darker world
Was home to more haters

Than innovators;

A world that Green
Had never seen
For he had never been

Trapped in a Tight-Lid-Jar Society.

Boy caught a fly
And gave trapping
Green a try.

But Green was too smart
And knew what it was like
To be free

Never lived life in a Tight-Lid-Jar Society.

EPICS 2: Spy Included

So at the speed of light
Green jumped onto a tree
And out of the way and out of sight.

Boy was awed by Green's might
For Green was a little frog
Who could easily fit in Boy's Tight-Lid-Jar.

Green jumped from tree to tree;
For all he wanted to be
Was free.

Boy was as fast as he could be;
With Tight-Lid-Jar in hand,
He ran into foreign land.

The minutes turned into hours
As Green jumped
Over many flowers.

Boy followed Green;
Carrying his Tight-Lid-Jar;
Both Green and Boy had travelled far.

III

As day turned into night
Boy felt paralyzing fright
For this was his first time

That he had been so alone
Under the stars
So far from home.

So Boy leaned against a log
In the Bog;
A nice place for a frog.

And Boy fell asleep.
Boy's Momma thought the worse;
Hoped Boy was not a victim of someone perverse.

Green was now in a different part of town;
And nothing seemed the same,
His bog, his log

Things that make a home for a frog
Were no longer in sight;
And Green too felt paralyzing fright;

EPICS 2: Spy Included

As Green awoke in a tree
Girl tried to give Green a kiss
Hoping Green would turn into a prince.

Girl's kiss was a miss
As startled Green
Jumped so high

Even though Green could not fly
All he could see
Was the sky.

He landed on the other side of town.
The side of town
Which was run down

People were rushing here and there
All avoiding eyes
Green had never seen so many feet

Green was hungry and needed something to eat
He saw a fly on a piece of meat
And Green took the opportunity to feast

At times Green was just another beast
Yanked by the hunger felt by all
Living on the food chain

Made everyone feel so small
When poverty's pull yanked too tight
Men once standing tall, would soon crawl.

Now Green felt so alone;
As all the feet were rushing by;
Green felt homeless and started to cry.

It came too fast for Green to know;
The time which was his to die.
When he was crushed

By all the rushed;
Green's life
Had just gone by.

THE END

CULTURAL GENOCIDE

#19. CULTURAL GENOCIDE

I

There was nowhere
For Chee to hide
Dee Stole her pride

For Chee loved Dee
Dee did not feel the same
Cultural Genocide

Psychic Suicide

No use for guns and knives
When fear and beer
Can just as easily ruin lives.

There are bars that can bind you;
Bars that confine you;
They even have bars of love

Full of hate
Bars that trap; control fate;
Contained too much distraction

Chee remembered her True Love too late.

EPICS 2: Spy Included

The music got her heart pounding
She felt feelings she never felt before
And just wanted more

The pleasure
Grew to be astounding
Before she fell to the floor

An illusion
Of make believe
Stole the innocence to cry for

Lost life
To die for
The war that never used a gun

Chee thought it would be fun
But her true love was not there
The only one who would ever care

Chee awoke in a brain drain
Now the ancient chain
Linked Chee to the system

Cultural Genocide
The pain
Caused Chee's Psychic Suicide.

One side takes all
Trying to integrate
Led to Chee's fall

No one cared or heard her scream
For her true love was not there
Too far away; in another land

Not even close to hold her hand;
And what was left of love was forgotten
Chee's Hopelessness felt too rotten

Lost identity
Took over her mind
How could Chee really see

That Dee had grown unkind

You can't go far
If you don't know
Who you are

A dirty way to fight
Which turned Chee's world
Upside down

Cultural Genocide
Progressed as Dee spoke
With a forked tongue

Hurt Chee more
Than any
Gun

II

Chee tried too hard
As each door slammed in her face
No one wanted to see her in any place

Chee tried so hard
Just to smile
While the well to do

Looked right through Chee
As if she wasn't there
And Chee's Pain just grew.

The only thing free for Chee
Was beer; a gift from someone perverse
Then things only got worse

III

How can anyone look away during the overkill
While the underfed
Are dying in all this greed.

While they bulldoze
Affordable housing
All over town

Nowhere to grow
Many abandoned tomorrow
Lost in fear and sorrow

Nowhere to belong
Nowhere to eat
To grow strong

Too easy to feel defeat.

Cultural Genocide
Psychic Suicide
Lost pride

Nowhere to hide
Such a fine line
That keeps one sane

Fine line to block the pain
Fine like between the Haves and Have Nots
Fine line too easily broken

Then the pain will be awoken
Fine line; do not cross;
For the fine line is the boss

The line Chee was not allowed to cross
Nowhere to belong
Nowhere to eat

Chee felt defeat
Chee hoped for love
But they sexualized her

She looked for hope
But all they gave her
Were false leads and rope

In a fool's game
Where no one bleeds
Out in the open

Very few
Remember Chee's name
Most treat with disdain

Cultural Genocide
Psychic Suicide
Chee wanted to belong

They all said that she was wrong

The man wearing the boots
Told Chee to move along
Brought a tear to her eye

Chee wondered if it was better just to die

The current in the wire was moving higher
And when Chee climbed to the top
The wire cut her

Barbed and so sharp
Broken flesh could only bleed
And weaken Chee

IV

Lee started a business hoping to thrive
Soon the building fell apart
Stu's indifference broke Lee's heart.

A bird made a nest
In the hole in the wall
And sang a song to soothe Lee's mind

While the world turned an eye
The bird remembered the parking lot
As a meadow so green

Now full of cars; the beauty could not be seen.

Parking for an hour or two was all that was allowed
The attendant wouldn't be back
For the rest of the day

So all those cars were allowed to stay.

Lee saw the attendant after five
He congratulated Lee
For keeping his business alive

In the climate of cultural genocide
Lee borrowed as much money as anyone can
Hoping to have the same chance

As any other man;
Then what should appear
A no entry sign and just more fear;

As debt accumulated;
Barriers just denigrated
And divided the town

Between the Haves and Have Nots
It had always been that way
They say

Rich get richer
As the poor get poorer
Cultural Genocide

Affordable housing
Was bulldozed away
For those shacks were in the way

They were blocking the view
For the well to do
In a place were only few could belong

Chee tried to be strong
They said she was wrong
When Chee was just trying too get along

V

They bow to the thing
And all the power that money can bring
But heaven help the ones called Lee and Chee

Without a penny to their name
They will be the ones to blame
Where they stand will grow into a frame

Hate mongering
Fear mongering
With nowhere to hide

Cultural Genocide
Psychic Suicide
Lost in a world

That could be undone
If we stood as one
All together; under one sun;

That spherical flaming entity
Way up there
Power for all to share

Anchored so diligently
In the sky
Hope gave courage

So Lee and Chee gave it another try

EPICS 2: Spy Included

As they stood below
Fusion power so mighty
They hoped to grow

A better tomorrow
For the sun
Was beginning to shine

And a day had just begun

Blinding to the naked eye
Divine Hotness on show
So much we will never know

The Sun brought life
While water fed it
During all of this misery

Blessed; ancient; mystery.

So you and I, could grow
In Paradise not really lost
Just behind a golden gate

Controls fate
Stirs up hate
Cultural Genocide

Psychic Suicide

The mightiest power of all
One day will be
Pure balance would soon reclaim

And will know Chee and Lee's name
Then all would be well
Once Lee and Chee escaped this Hell.

THE END

GLUE

#20 GLUE

I

The Bubble was about to pop
The bottom was about to drop
The clock was about to stop

Lines were forming
The air was warming
The Ozone level was rising

The whole world appeared to be uprising;

The Bubble overvalued things
The trouble had just begun
The rubble was everywhere

For Money Front-runners
Had swept the land;
We were all under Storm-Man's command.

We tried not to forget the power of our love
For it was stronger than any glue;
Brighter than any star

EPICS 2: Spy Included

Far above every war
Could heal the deepest scar
Would defy those willing to lie.

We walked by a long line
Outside the Money Mart.
Rolling out stuff

In a grocery cart
It was a bad start
And our future was up in air

So much wasn't fair.

Gated; Poverty so legislated
Too little measured;
Too much speculated;

Branded; all we had was our True Love.

Our Love would try to unify;
And free us from bias
Negative response loop;

Storm-Man's negative pull;
Was said to be the new social science
Zero tolerance for defiance;

For Storm-Man was a political predator
Social Speculator
And ruled with an iron fist;

While the list of the missing debtors grew.

Storm-Man's blood lust was showing
With gun in hand he manufactured our consent
We heard many had been buried in cement.

Storm-Man told us how to live;
And told Momma
When to die;

We knew the power of our Love was true;
For it was brighter than any star;
Far above every war;

Would heal the deepest scar.

II

True love
Mending in unity
True Love giving us new opportunity;

Empowering every community;
Even when Faded Brown Shirted Storm-Man
Appeared from the past.

The Money Front-runners were in charge

While a positive feed-back loop
Took a life of its own
While Storm-Man

Political Predator;
Another social speculator
Touched every debtor

With their heart of stone.

Storm-Man was protected by Impunity
Culture of Obstruction
To displace Opportunity.

Nasty Devolution
Pushing; Shoving;
Never loving

Told us where to stand
While we waited
They looked at us as if we were hated

Gated in poverty that was legislated
Too little measured;
Too much was speculated;

While the Bubble was bursting
Many of us were hurting
Even though we knew

True Love would get us through
For it was brighter than any star
Far above every war

Could heal every scar
That was branding us
In unforgiving bias

Nasty Devolution

Culture of Obstruction
Like Glue
Kept us stuck to the past;

Political Predator
Social Speculator
Holding us back

Refusing to hear

Trapped in a culture of fear;
Just another invisible hand
Manipulating supply and demand

Across the land.

Gated by Legislated Poverty
And Hatred
Too little measured

Too much speculated;
Sheltered by Impunity
Storm-Man; political predator

From the past
Had returned
Many dropped dead before they had learned;

Lost Opportunity

Nasty Devolution
While we knew True Love
Was the only cure;

For True Love would always shine
Brighter than any star
Far above every war

Could heal the deepest scar.

And we knew
Safety was in our Unity;
And True Love would find a way;

To energize us;
Keep us strong
While the world was going wrong.

EPICS 2: Spy Included

The Bubble was bursting
Opening the floor
As value sunk into the bottomless pit

Some called the Abyss
Others called it
An Opportunity missed.

As Storm-Man
Was empowered by the Devolution
He could put us in a slot;

He could order us to be shot;

Nasty Devolution
Shaped who we could be
While Storm-Man was granted Impunity

We had all our stuff
In a grocery cart
Walking past lines at the Money Mart
Our True Love would always shine

Brighter than any star
Far above every war
Would heal the deepest scar

As Culture of Obstruction got in the way
Made us miss
Another Opportunity.

III

Faded Brown Shirted Storm-Man

Political Predator
Social Speculator
Was kicking his boots

Stared and glared with bias which was oozing
We had all of our stuff in a shopping cart
Went by a long line

Outside the Money Mart
Then we hid in the park
Once it was dark

Mind Shaker
Grave Digger
Goal Breaker

For a few hundred dollars an hour
Gated Legislated Poverty
Made us feel hated

While the Bubble was getting ready to burst.

IV

We hold on
To our dream
Of True love

So we have something to believe in
Which is brighter than any star
Far above every war

Where opposite sides are seen no more.
In reality we fight to survive.
We were put on a list

Said we were missing
Though we were behind that Tree
Hiding from Storm-Man

With all our stuff
In a grocery cart
As the line outside the Money Mart

Was growing
As the Bubble was bursting in spurts
We knew many would be getting hurt.

We could not speak out, we were not free,
Did not want to be taken away
To a place where we would have no say.

We knew our capture would create a good job for the few;
For the rest of us
We dreamed of a love that would be true.

EPICS 2: Spy Included

A love that would unite us
Not force us to fight
For our rights under bias

While the Bubble was so inflated
It was about to pop
And the clock was about to stop

Many would go mad
And jump from their roof top
Many would be left newly poor

While Storm-Man would be in his domain

As the bottom of the market sank
The Abyss came to light
Gave many a terrible fright

And we saw it all

As we hid behind that Holy Tree
Storm-Man could not see
Where we were

You know the Tree

That lived through
Different times of war
As it grew

We knew
True Love would never die
For it was brighter than any star

Far above every war
Could heal the deepest scar
After Storm-Man had his way.

Took over our ground
Nasty Devolution
True Love was the only solution;

Our hope
Was said to be
Mind pollution.

Turned Love into a bad word
So we called Love God
Because Hate was growing into the Destroyer.

Birth and decay
Luck and the unknown
Needed some Magical Thinking.

V

Storm-Man
Protected by Impunity;
Toxifying our Opportunity

Showing off his Hypocrisy

Feeling more important than you and me;
Tripping over his power lacking legitimacy
Before the fall

A list was made
Of debtors gone missing
But we were hiding behind that Tree

We all knew where we were;
The Faded Brown Shirted Storm-Man
Would try to break our bond in two

But we knew the power
Of our Love was true
It was mightier than glue

And could not be broken;
For we knew our True Love
Would shine brighter than any star

Far above every war;
Would heal
The deepest scar.

Our True Love would be always mending;
Our hurt inside kept us bending;
As we hung our heads low.

Storm-Man
Ordered us about
Sounded like a drone;

He knew we were alone

His droning was Mind numbing
And he was slow
That is why we kept low.

VI

The boom was good
For many; it was true;
The Frenzy felt so right

As the Bubble inflated
And grew
Around me and you

Some said the Bubble
Would burst suddenly
Which was why Storm-Man

Brought fear here;
Arrived so fast;
He was summoned from the past;

He would have watched us all day
But that Tree was in the way
And Bird sang so happily

For new life just hatched that was family.
While the Bubble was bursting
We saw many lining up by the banks

Nasty Devolution
Political Predator
Social Speculator

Down to a science
Zero tolerance for defiance
As the Money Front-runners

Touched every debtor

With their heart of stone.
As we searched
For opportunity we felt so alone.

As we pushed all of our stuff in a grocery cart
We went by the long line
Outside the Money Mart

Storm-Man
Was standing in our way
While we were stereotyped

In hype for his force of external greed
We would not be weakened by our need
For we had our True Love by our side.

The cost of the Bubble bursting was out of sight
We knew our True Love
Was meant to unite

While Storm-Man

Sold what he could;
Sad man;
Weak man;

Never knew
What the power
Of love could do.

For he was a Liquidator
Just another Hater
For Profit.

The Bubble was bursting
Pushed prices through the floor
And into the Abyss

The bank was closed, the CEO had locked the door.

As the Bubble was bursting
Storm-Man yelled and screamed
He was protecting someone's revenue stream

Before he pushed some of us into his bottomless pit.

And True Love
Would link us hand in hand
All across

Our Mother Land

And Free us
From Storm-Man's Pull
As the Bubble was bursting all around.

VII

We knew
Our Love so true
Would get us through

The lies.
We knew our Love would energize
Grow into a great Power to behold

The new gold.
And we knew our love would
Show us the way.

Storm-Man
Was very angry indeed
For his hunger left him in constant need.

While the Bubble was bursting
He was frowning; pounding;
While we waited for the clock to stop ticking.

The floor above the abyss began to drop
Storm-Man demanded more profit
As many more were pushed into the bottomless pit.

Storm-Man was no longer lost in time;
He screamed,
He was still heartless and mean;

Overvalued assets
Made many feel richer than they were
Which inflated the Bubble even more

As competition was ran out of town;

They left silently, never causing a scene.
For Storm-Man
Was a weak man

A sad man

Lost his faith a long time ago
In Love so True
His heart grew bitter.

And we all knew
True Love was brighter than any star
Far above every war;

Could heal the deepest scar.
Would end oppression
Turn around negative suggestion.

Help share our common ground
Standing as one
Under one Sun

The bond of Love
Would make us one;
As we found a way to feed

Those dying in all this greed.
As the Bubble was bursting
Love would help us rise to our feet;

Would heal the deepest scar.

Storm-Man
Was so afraid of those he persecuted
He demanded them to be executed.

Prejudicial, No need for magical thinking

Storm-Man preferred to get us
Mindlessly drinking
For he needed us weaker than he

So he could manufacture
Our consent more freely
In this world; some called Paradise Lost

The true opportunity cost.

VIII

True Love was real
Willing and able,
To be as strong as love could be;

EPICS 2: Spy Included

Unifying loose ends;
Needing no amends;
Glued in True Love;

We were meant to unify then die.

Love was a giant jar of glue;
Power; when no one knew what to do;
A flower; blooming where ever it can

As trust bound the Rights of Man
Broken in war
Broken pieces all over the floor

Sinking into the Abyss
As the Bubble was breaking
The ground was shaking.

Trust glued some bonds back together again
The bonds were strong
Held us together for times so long.

Glued as one
One world, one life
While Storm-Man demanded a Negative Response Loop

Demanded more strife.

IX

We grow at life in trust
For we must
Dream

Today is the bridge
Between Yesterday and Tomorrow
Elevating and bonding

Ending all sorrow
True Love was the glue
That we knew would bond us as one.

Storm-Man tried to put an end
To our positive response loop;
Storm-Man wanted control.

He wanted his negative loop to dominate
Would cause hate
To vibrate.

He would smile while
Impunity paid the bill;
For the Faded Brown Shirted Storm-Man

EPICS 2: Spy Included

Was a liquidator
Just another hater
Waiting for the day

The Bubble would burst;
Out of sight
The floor above the Abyss

Would drop

Old rulers die hard;
Death was only days away;
And we knew our True Love

Was brighter than any star;
Far beyond every war;
Would heal the deepest scar.

A better destiny for sure
True Love was the only cure.
The Glue to bond us as one

Under one Sun.

X

True Love was forgotten
Not by us
But by those who had everything money could buy;

And needed nothing more
As the Bubble was bursting
The Abyss had opened its floor.

Deep below
Was the bottomless pit
So the ones thrown in could fit.

The Liquidator
Social Speculator
Touched every debtor

With their heart of stone.

While shedding crocodile tears;
Never looking at us
In the eye.

"And without True Love
All the hurt could not be forgotten,"
Hope cried out again.

Storm-Man
Will fool them again!
While they look away

Many will be pushed into the Bottomless Pit
As the Abyss
Opens the door.

Another Liquidation
Another hurt sensation
Watching Storm-Man scream
Our dream away

So many pushed
Into the other side;
Making money feeds Storm-Man's pride;

Storm-Man will tell them how to live;
And tell their Momma when to die;
He will turn away when they cry.

Just another war crime
Before our time;
The ghosts of yesterday wanted to stay."

True Love replied to Hope;
"Yes, I will make you stronger
Then it will be easier to cope."

"I know you, True Love,
Will do what you can
But how do you soften

Faded Brown Shirted Storm-Man?
Another liquidator;
Waiting for the Floor to drop

Just another hater, another goal breaker;
Pushing who he can into
The Bottomless Pit."

And True Love replied
"We have you, Hope,
And you strengthen me.

As long as I have you, I shall never die."
Hope replied.
"Some say

True Love is the road to suicide.

But we know the opposite is true;
We know what we must do
To free the people from Storm-Man's reign;

We must unite; go beyond the pain;
Love and Hope, together, so electrifying;
Before the Bubble bursts.

How do we forgive Storm-Man?
He defames who he can.
We knew our true love would find a way.

We knew our True Love
Was brighter than any star
Far above every war

Would heal the deepest scar.

And we knew too
Hope and True Love
Would unite.

Showed us strength
We never knew we had;
And then we felt no fear;

So we didn't feel so sad.
We were able to forgive
And our strength grew

That was when we knew
That the power of Love was really true
And was deep in our hearts

Buried in the dark
While we slept in the park
As the Faded Brown Shirted Storm-Man

Militarized everything in sight
Belted out his might
Caused us a terrible fright.

XI

Storm-Man
Had a billing code slot
For everything that wasn't shot

Hope waited Her turn
Then held True Love's hand.
"Yes I know all about You

You, so True, you are my Inspiration.
Mystical; magical;
Ancient sensation

For the last generation
Without a home
Nowhere to roam

Shielded behind our positive response loop
Storm-Man
Pulled out his loop of negativity

We could feel it drone
It was so near
We felt so much fear.

We tried to stand up for what was right
With enough strength and courage
To let live

But that only started a fight
That we could never win
While our True Love

Was called a sin
We knew our True Love would unite
And glow brighter than any star

Shining above every war
Healing the deepest scar
As our True Love grew

It would stay glued; stronger than tar;
As manufactured war, famine and drought;
We knew Storm-Man had too much clout.

We wanted to be free
Form his power of negativity
Starvation, division and confusion;

EPICS 2: Spy Included

As the Bubble was bursting
We let our True Love bloom
Hoping it would take us beyond

Exclusion and doom."
True Love replied,
After she cried.

"We must never be confined
Or be a slave to any master mind
For the world needs us now

More than ever before.

For we,
You and me
Hope and Love,

Work best as one
Under one Sun
Stronger than glue.

Working together
For millennia
Stronger than any militia

Though we know
We better grow faster,"
Hope said with a sigh;

"I see the new age of hysteria
Arriving as the Bubble is bursting."
Hope tried not to cry.

XII

Love and Hope glued us as one
Connecting and mending
Love and Hope were spread all around;

Divided no more;

Found common ground;
Felt our mass heart pound;
The skin drum sent signals of sound;

Yes it is true
We were alive
We had survived

As we could hear the echoes

Of the overkilling
Of the underfed
Storm-Man found it thrilling.

Love would mend broken hearts
That were torn apart
And make them whole again

Love would bond stronger than glue
Make us as one
Under one Sun

That shines so bright
When no clouds are in the way
Regardless of what was done that day.

Love's Bond could glue
And mend every heart
That had been torn apart

For we knew
That Love so True
Was brighter than any star

Far above every war
Would heal the deepest scar."
And Hope agreed.

I hugged the Tree
So near to me
And hoped

The Faded Brown Shirted Storm-Man
Did not see
For I needed a good vibration

To face the world that day.

XIII

We are born into this world
So broken and torn;
Only Love's glue could help it mend

Show us when to bend;
While Storm-Man
Militarized and liquidated

All he could;
Things began to rust;
And there was a loss of human trust;

It was true; we felt hated.

EPICS 2: Spy Included

We knew it was getting late
And fate was around the bend
We needed to mend.

Broken lines were everywhere
So many; we didn't care.
Some lines were manufactured to divide us;

Some just to antagonize us;
We had plenty of reason to hide
As we held on to the Tree.

The Bubble was bursting
The bottom had opened into a bottomless pit
And nothing could be free

We knew our love so true was the only way
For it was brighter than any star
Far above ever war

And would heal the deepest scar.

Our feet were free to roam;
And we knew we might never have a home;
Living our days misunderstood;

We were rejected
And now free
To raise the pillars

In a dark world of killers
Our pillars absorbed the shock
We grew; for we were still young;

And we were
To build the new world
That was promised a long time ago.

For we had the Glue
And the First Pillar
Was absorbing the shock.

"We gave it all that we got,"
Hope and Love said at once
Storm-Man was clicking his boots.

XIV

We were running out of time;
We had witnessed Storm-Man's crime;
We had a long way to climb;

For Devolution; manufactured consent;
Left many buried in cement;
And many more were pushed into the bottomless pit

As the Bubble was bursting.

While Storm-Man
Was liquidating and intimidating;
We all ran away.

XV

While we were coping;
And saving
Whatever we could.

We did not know
The many who were shot;
We knew there had been a lot.

The Macro Power
Over-lorded the Micro
Even though Micro was the core;

The Bubble was still bursting

XV

Micro and the Macro were one
Needed glue;
For the world was so broken;

And could have been whole
As one
Under One Sun

And the implosion
Opened the floor
Just like before

And many were pushed into the pit;
Liquidated, intimidated;
We knew there was a better way.

We found the strength to forgive;
And did the best
We could to live;

For we knew
What True Love could do;
It was brighter than any star;

Far above every war
Light enough
To heal the deepest scar

Made us one
Under one Sun
As the building of the new world

Had just begun.

THE END

SPY

#21. SPY

I

Some said they had to forgive
So they could let some joy live
Under the setting sun

Glowing over
Failed City
Still so pretty

In the morning sun too
Many were poor
But didn't feel blue

Their time had not yet come to an end
So the persecuted rose to their feet
Always staying on their side of the street

Not yet polluted, the mouth of the mighty river
Welcomed larvae carried by ocean currents;
As time flew

The larvae grew
Into fish
Big enough to eat

Free from body politics
So confining
And mind numbing

The eagles flourished
Living in the giant trees
While the flowers nearby

Attracted honey bees.
Puffy said
"I am master to all this."

Puffy built a fence to keep
All the nature in
And the uninvited out.

The excluded didn't cry and didn't shout
Some said they had to forgive
So they could let some joy live

EPICS 2: Spy Included

Under the setting sun
Glowing over
Failed City
Still so pretty

Puffy, was one of many elected officials;
Lost effectiveness; Lost legitimacy
Though no one knew for sure

What came first
The Failing City;
Or the Failing Puffy

Sat on a rock
He was in shock
Failing city

Was still so pretty

Able to defy
Common sense
Puffy did not control petty expense

So locked into rules to protect fools;

The persecuted were feared;
For they looked so hungry all the time;
Puffy declared that they were unfit to live;

And the well to do agreed
So caught they were
In their greed

To some, Fear was might,
To others Forgiveness made things right,
Everyone could agree

It would take a lot of love
To prevent
World War III

As the autocracy
And mind numbing bureaucracy
Declared that Failing City

Was the happiest place of all
Though only the well to do
Need to drop by to have a ball

EPICS 2: Spy Included

Hate and Love still lived; setting passions on fire;

Puffy praised all
The wealth
That he had under his command

He kneeled before the Invisible Hand
That was said to be touching everything in the land
And was the only force that seemed to care.

Puffy wasn't self-aware
And we were on our guard
Living in separate worlds

Was the only way
We could survive
To never let them into our minds

We had two faces
The one we showed to those we owed
And our own

We were unbroken
Though our pain had awoken
We were young enough

To have a heart full of love.
The visible bopping heads projected
A world divided and unfair
As the river raged

The sun was hidden
As the rain came in torrents
And soaked into the ground

The bopping heads would not listen to warnings
That the raging river
Was eroding the dyke

In the river's bend
Even though Puffy's home
Was standing there behind the fence

To keep all the nature in
And all the uninvited out
As the river raged freely

Beyond the power of the ‘Well To Do’.

Puffy said
The Dyke could be managed
For another day

And told the engineers to move on
As the ‘Well To Do’ continued to project
Their day away so freely

Sitting in Failing City;
The Dyke would was not built
To hold back the super-flood’s raging waters

Many avoided the town
Said it was the city of doom
Decaying too fast;

As Puffy sat on his wall
The engineers predicted
That he would have a very great fall

While the collective mind of the well to do
Was living in the past;
So their autocratic power could last

We kept low
Tried not to show
Everything we know;

Projecting at will for a thrill
Words taken out of context
For a fight; they did it all night;

Too close for comfort, and too far away to communicate;
The policy function was never executed
Lost opportunity to integrate

Lost channel to communicate

Policy never lived through the day
And was buried
Under bad news

Puffy was so ineffective,
He sat on the wall
And everyone knew

That he was going to have a great fall.

Jethro and Bill were hired
To put things back together again
Failing City was broken into two parts

The 'Have Nots' and the 'Well To Do';

Lived as if there was a wall in between
When they met; they never spoke
Prevented a scene;

Some tried to smile
And were accused
Of substance abuse

As the barrier's reflection
Pushed out those
Who tried to get into the door

They were told that they weren't wanted no more.
Some had a lot
Others were doomed to be a Have Not;

Forced to live
In squalor and rot
As the 'Well To Do' claimed and framed

Within their self-serving projection
They were paid to project all day
Good Job; Good Pay;

Standing on their Pedestal
Was their favorite thing to do;
Looking down; wearing a frown;

As their neighbor's house
Was burning down;
They fought over words

In the usual way
And they had nothing much
More to say

Injury to our community
Was done on our side of the fence
We forgave; Easier to behave;

EPICS 2: Spy Included

We were not broken
Still young enough
To have a heart full of love

Out of time
Out of sync
The loss was hidden in black ink

Whispers spoken not meant to be heard
By anyone like me and you
Such was the power to be elite

So entitled to stand on their feet;
We too refused to be broken;
While the fire raged;

The water tower
Had been sold
No one was told

We heard the whispering;
Manufactured words so decisive
If they were trying for peace

It would have been malpractice
To demoralize and criticize;
Would never break the ice

That was what Global Warming was for

We refused to be broken
We had our two faces
We knew we could survive

As long as we stayed alive
We too would stand on our feet
We too would not fade away

Or die in all this greed;

As the deer ran by; we saw them hide;
Before they were shot;
Which was done a lot;

Just like us
We were trapped on a slot
So easily shot;

EPICS 2: Spy Included

Road kill by any other name
Would have been sad
And called a shame

But many could not see
Behind the fence
Built to keep the nature in

And the uninvited out
Jethro and Bill
Were having another barbecue

And the fire was very hot;

Meaning of what was said
Was relative
To how we had to live

We were silent
In ear shot
And hid

For we were unbroken
Our pain had awoken
But we had our two faces to survive

And we were so thankful to still be alive

We were still young enough
To have a heart
Full of love

What we were able to give
Was so energizing
And satisfying

More than just a voice in our head
Which was never allowed to speak
Was meant to keep us weak

Conscience was flaming before the fall
The Humpty Dumpties
Were sitting on their wall

They wanted it all;

EPICS 2: Spy Included

Thought the rules
To protect fools
Could protect them

From the River's might.
The rules of fear
Made it hard to hear

The words of the engineer
Said many times before
That the riverbanks were eroding

And the dyke would not hold
The water rushing through
At the river's bend

The dyke needed to be reconstructed soon
Or the Failing City; So pretty;
Glowing under the setting sun

Was doomed
For the dyke
Would not hold

And the trees
Soaking so much water
Had been sold

The dyke could not hold
During a Super Flood
The ground would turn to mud.

And the war of words had just begun
As the Have Nots
Were pushed out of the door

No need for you to be here
You are too poor
Come back when you have more

We are still the Promised Land
Touched
By the Invisible Hand

So they could project all day
About people
Who had no say

Good Job; Good Pay;

Living in a land
That used to grow plenty
Now was running on empty

As the Early Birds flew away

We would not be broken
Though our pain had awoken
We were young enough

To have a heart full of love.

II

And how we tried
To defy all the stereotypes and lies;
Hypocrisy; too willfully blind to see;

Sometimes they knew our names;
We did not count;
We were living on the other side of the tracks;

We did not even know how to play their games;

We were Subject Material
For projecting into words
So Mystical and Prejudicial

No Entry Point
To connect into
No interface to grow

Failing City

Some of us were debtors; some of us were owed;
Many of us had nowhere to park
So we were all towed;

Making way for a bike lane
Too green to be mean
Lost under snow

Marginalized and disenfranchised
Always subject material
For projection

EPICS 2: Spy Included

As Jethro and Bill
Flew above us; in the air;
Good Job; Good Pay;

We had nowhere to go
As cars were pulled into a lot beside the Money Mart
Both places always cost a lot.

As we poor, grew poorer,
The rich grew in stature;
They stood hand in hand, on their pedestal,

While Humpty Dumpty sat on his wall;
Some looked away
Knowing there would be a fall

For all the rules in the land
Could not protect such fools;
From Fate.

For Cruelty Ruled
And we knew why.
We young were kicked down

And learned not to cry
In Failing City
Broken in Two

We were the other half
Wearing the outside face
As we roamed from place to place;

There was no way back
We We knew we were spoken about behind our backs
For we were born on the wrong side
Of the Railway Track

Related by blood and that was all
And once down on our luck

We had to crawl
Through Sprawl
As our fear continued to grow

Many forgot to plan for tomorrow
Failing City, no economic viability
For it had so little virility

III

The young were run out of town
So another Humpty Dumpty could wear the crown
As he sat on his wall; he frowned;

EPICS 2: Spy Included

Puffy's assistants; Jethro and Bill
Had a secret thrill
And it was to barbecue,

Sometimes in a meadow
So green,
Not often ever seen.

Where Free Spirits
Thought they could live
Until they were ready to die

While Jethro and Bill
Were flying
High in the sky

Their next biggest thrill
Was to interfere
With anyone near

And in sight
For they were in full flight
Though they would always stop

For Barbeque

These surveillance men in the sky
Had many things to do
We all knew that was true;

Whenever there was a chance nearby
Jethro and Bill
Would take time off

To hunt for barbeque
A secret thrill
For Jethro and Bill

They knew when to hide from Puffy

Who ruled Failing City by fear;
Hired these surveillance men,
Hoping intelligence was always near;

Good Job; Good Pay;

EPICS 2: Spy Included

To watch the mob;
From the air;
Way up there;

Jethro and Bill always found the time
To stop for Barbeque
When opportunity met their eye

So much to see
When they were
Flying high in the sky

No right to privacy
As far as we can see
In Failing City;

Too rigid to be
Fluid
Moving against the flow of time.

IV

What a thrill
For Jethro and Bill
To take photos of everything in sight

Made it harder for us to think
Let alone dream
Made some want to scream

Once our guard was down
Our vulnerability set in;
That was the time Jethro and Bill would intrude

Announcing on their one way speaker radio
That we were all rude and the 'Well To Do'
Wanted us to go;

For they blamed us for their failing town
Blamed us for bringing them down;
Some said ventilation and unfair speculation

Made good projection for all

And that was before the fall
When Humpty Dumpty fell off the wall
Jethro and Bill saw it all;

It was their role
For mind control;
Good Job; Good Pay;

Jethro and Bill
Let nothing else
Get in the way

The years went by
Some were born
And some were given permission to die

Without even asking why.

Danger was in the air
And everywhere
But Jethro and Bill

Didn't care
Too busy looking for Barbeque
While surveilling me and you.

Jethro and Bill
Were fired on the Spot
When Puffy's finances grew too hot

And Puffy was found to be

Caught up in a terrible controversy
When spending could no longer be justified
As political

Puffy tried using words that were mystical

V

Jethro and Bill's new job
Was the same as their old job
To marginalize and criticize

Sometimes in disguise

EPICS 2: Spy Included

And always to survey
Made us obey
Watching so high in the sky

Good Job; Good Pay;
Never got in the way of their hunt though
For Barbeque was never too hidden

And never forbidden;

Vulnerability;
Of Momma Deer To Be
Was a fact; naturally;

She tried so hard to avoid; Human contact;

She stood still
Hoping for a higher will
To leave her unbroken

Meanwhile
Jethro and Bill loved the thrill of the kill
Remained their favorite thing to do

Equal to surveying everyone everywhere
From the air
Without a care.

Looking at us as if we had no right to be there.

As they flew in the sky
A cloud of Happy Drink
Would flow into our stream

Some started to scream
And never knew why
Then they were given permission to die.

Jethro and Bill
Knew their job well
And it was to hunt us down

And to kick us out of town

EPICS 2: Spy Included

For we were the 'Have Nots'
And the price of realestate
Was about to crash

Would leave many
Without any cash
And we were blamed for Failing City

Never elected at all;
Narrow scope of vision;
Poisoned by suspicion;

Only ones allowed to make a decision;

As the eye and the pie in the sky
Were circling us from the air
We knew the line

For it too was written
From the sky
Told us what to do; everyday;

In every way;

How to live; and when to die
And what to say on the way
Manufacturing consent day by day.

As Jethro and Bill flew by
Looking for barbecue
From the sky.

And to survey
One day; to make us obey
In some degrading way;

Like you know who.
But first Jethro and Bill
Wanted the thrill of Barbecue.

VI

We never knew when
The bulldozers would come
But we knew it would be some day

We hoped many years from now.
Still we knew the bulldozers
Were on their way

EPICS 2: Spy Included

While Jethro and Bill
Were having a thrill
Doing Barbeque

Waiting in line;
Every day for everything;
Life in Failed City

Was a waiting game;
Interrupted
By random cues;

Often inflating
IOUs;
Felt so dehumanizing for me and you.

We would soon be dispossessed
Were hoping that life
Could bring on the best

Soon we realized the trap
Of concrete everywhere
As Jethro and Bill

Flew in the air
Above
Nothing was about love

Jethro and Bill
Looked right through me and you
For they were hunting

For Barbecue

In the other part of town
So many
Felt so down

Waiting in soon to be Bulldozed homes
Have Nots faced the barrier of concrete unknowns
For they were just paying rent

And the plan was to sell the land
To retired folk from out of town
Who would be easy to command.

"Move in
Win win
You will love the view

EPICS 2: Spy Included

So much to do;
For Jethro and Bill
Surveying in the air

Watching us
As we try to do chores
Visit the stores.

While it was getting warmer
Day by day;
So Barbeque was always on its way."

Puffy wrote a message for the nation
The speech lacked sensation
Puffy had little imagination

Though projection was his strength
He always said
And the ones who objected

Were only slaves to the voices in their collective head
Puffy said many times a day
Good job; Good Pay;

"Silence is better," that is what Puffy said;
We were denied common sense;
While his culture of obstruction; forced confusion;

So external;

Always a peril
For every living thing
Even for the rabbits

Living in the rabbit hole

Where Momma rabbit made a home
Under concrete and stone
It was her own

Her family was content
Though some called her a pest
She tried her best

To stay unbroken.

The message to bore
Was sent with great speed
So loud; could not be ignored.

Message broadcasted from the air.
People heard the word;
And thought all would be right;

Until they too were surveilled
All through the night;
Then it just didn't feel right;

But made the well to do
Feel braver
And safer.

VII

Sometimes Jethro and Bill
Would fly into Myria
To spy from the air on those living there.

To fight a force no one would name
Though it was the force
Everyone was to blame.

The genteel crowd was happy all the same
They owned their home
While the displaced

Were still free to roam

Slept all over the place
But the genteel crowd
Looked away

And summoned the list
Where complainers could meet
They loved to micro-managed that way

Good for control
Which was the role
For the eye in sky

EPICS 2: Spy Included

Some say
We will die
When told; Still not too old;

Never too late
For such a fate;
Lost words; hidden in fear and hate;

Failed city
Where many were waiting
Until they were told to die.

On the other side of town
The poor were provoked
And to not to speak

They were so hungry and very weak

They phoned the authorities
To have them moved out of the way
And banned.

So they could see more land

They demanded roads
To be privatized
So only the chosen few

The 'Well To Do'
Would be entitled
To be there

Everyone else could be displaced
The 'Well To Do'
Didn't know their face

Living behind the fence
To keep all the nature in
And the uninvited out

So quick to draw conclusion
So slick they were fooled
By all the confusion

EPICS 2: Spy Included

The doggy eat doggy world
Had only
Just begun

While the failed city
Glowed
Under the setting sun

Advertised
As the happiest place around
As the torrents of rain

Could no longer soak into the ground

While many more Humpty Dumpties
Sat on the wall
Looking at it all

Watching the poor and the destitute crawl
But we were not broken
We knew they were going to fall

Out of sight
Was out of mind
While Jethro and Bill

Though they could see everything from the air

As re-construction of road furniture
Had just begun
On the poor side of town

No entry signs were put up
The sort that looked like delete
The poor were so hungry they had nothing to eat

The genteel crowd
Complained
Thought those rough folk

Should be detained
While it rained
The water could not soak into the ground

For too many trees had been cut down
Taken away
And sold in town.

EPICS 2: Spy Included

"The roads should be privatized,"
All the Humpty Dumpties said at once;
As they were getting ready to pounce;

Though the roads were paid for by the public purse
It was ruled by Puffy
So things just got worse

While the watchers; Jethro and Bill;
Watched us for money and thrill
Above Failing City

Below all Heavenly Bodies.
The Humpty Dumpties forced the landless to pay
For the poor and destitute had no say

The Humpty Dumpties
Had one way
And knew nothing more

They lived behind a fence
To keep the nature in
And the uninvited out.

We refused to be broken
Or to be frozen in Time.
We progressed the best we could;

Like our Papa's would;

So we all walked by
And went to the mall
Where all the merchants were renting the hall

Behind empty stores hidden
By a pretty paper wall
Puffy pointed to the crowd

As he read the rules Out loud
We knew the rules
Could not protect the fools

And we were not broken
Would not be demoralized
When criticize

For we were waiting for the fall
Never distracted
By the window dressing

In the Hall
In the Mall
Of the failing city

So pretty
When glowing
Under the setting sun.

VIII

Others asked if this should be
Government's role at all
Others were too afraid

To say anything before the Fall
And went on their way
Cherishing the silence

After filling out the form
Which was demanded of them
Whiles they could hear the hum

Of the surveillance men
Jethro and Bill
Who were flying in the sky

So they could look down on us
And watch us cry
While Public Officials gave us permission to die

After revealing our life
Out of context in Failing City
The story was never pretty

They embarrassed whoever they could
By putting their file so confidential
On the Net

EPICS 2: Spy Included

Some victims lost their joy of life
Though they were not dead yet
Felt they had nothing of value to give

Were told suicide was the only way

To deny this truth
Jethro and Bill said
One must be sick in the head

For they knew how to play the game;
The power to break another person's mind
The best job in town;

To intrude in someone's personal space
Was the domain of the Parties
In charge and quite large

Manufactured words to create despair
Demoralization
A hurt sensation

For the abandoned generation

So intense
And so experimental
And always so impersonally personal.

The job of the Surveillance Men
Jethro and Bill
Were looking down at us, from the air.

Without a care
To tear one off
Right off their feet

When Puffy lost his job
Jethro and Bill were given this role
And the means was called mind control

EPICS 2: Spy Included

Sometimes they wore Burghas
To hide their identity
But their shiny boots

And gun on hip
Gave them away
While we; the unbroken

And apologized in the usual way

We had been looking down
Saw those shiny boots and gun on hip
One more time again.

THE END

CRUSHED

#22. CRUSHED

I

Grumpy old men; counting their cash
See the pile; had time to grow;
Opportunities from the past

Leading into tomorrow

Grumpy Old Men count their cash
In front of their window
No common sense needed

Snobocrat
The new aristocrat
Staring at Us so suspiciously

As we walk by
They tell us what it will cost to live
And what it will cost to die;

Grumpy Old Men;
Rulers of the war tone zone;
Us; we were walking through; all alone.

Going against the flow
Of Time
For they are old and cold

We are young and hot
Always looking for a bright spot
So afraid of getting shot;

Us; just a moving dot on a scatterplot;
In the war tone zone;
For it is still a rich man's world.

And we are the forgotten sons
Of Grumpy Old Men
Growing footprints in the air

If they knew Us; we are sure they would care.
But they are too busy
Growing their footprints in the air.

We are put down and never let in
And there is nothing that we can see
Their dark space has no transparency.

II

Constitution; health of a nation
Born into this world
What a sensation

We are less tough when shown love;
Nowhere to go;
Just Us; locked inside this Chaos;

We all know
The power tree
Of this social ordered hierarchy

Some are put under house arrest
So they are not seen
Starving behind their locked door

The Old Way is now the New Way
Some say more true
Than ever before

Behind a locked door
Grumpy Old Men
Growing their footprints in the air.

The gap grows; we just get the glare;
We don't have a dime
Just a lot of time

No need for life's ambition
For there are no doors open to Us;
We are sneered at a lot

For we are just a moving dot
On a scatter plot
So afraid of getting shot;

While footprints grow in the air;
Manufactured fear is everywhere
Trapped inside this cosmic clock;

We are someone's forgotten son;
Our life's journey has just begun.
And we know we must stay free

For all things grow incrementally.
And confusion sets in when over-complicated baiters
Make profit as merciless haters.

EPICS 2: Spy Included

All about control; and we know;

We are less tough when shown love
Measuring risk
In a sensible way

Civilization
What a sensation
A bridge

Between generation
Living on this ancient world
Where Truth

Lives in every tree
So silently
Soaking in the bird's eye view

Of this Paradise
Lost; a long time ago
And we know

One day we will find
A place that we can call our own
Far away from this war tone zone.

Time
Extended for some
Stolen from others

Time

Linking the past with today
Finding a mutually beneficial way
Middle ground started to shake

We thought that we would break.

III

We are
Grumpy Old Men's forgotten sons.
And our life has just begun.

Secret meetings were all around
But Us; were never invited;
We never heard a sound.

IV

We had so little to defend;
Nothing to help Us mend.
We rose when we learned to bend.

Our journey was not yet to end.

Though we were left all alone
In the War Tone Zone
Their war.

Social Impact;
Fly by Night;
We hide when there is light.

We have grown to be elastic
For Grumpy Old hair dyed men
Try to shock Us with their static

While turning our world into plastic
Imprisoned in rules written by fools
Who can only win

If they stay in position; on top of the hill;
For a level playing field
Has no such thrill

Power
Corrupts some; it is True;
And many said we were blessed

Because we were dispossessed.

So persecuted in this land of fear;
They could never love Us;
Viscous circle; spinning around

Here in this War Tone Zone

And no one could see
But Truth
And Truth lived in every tree

Flew by
As a bird's eye
In the ever changing sky

V

This fence is long
Reminding Us
That we do not belong.

Lost connection
No home
We just roam.

EPICS 2: Spy Included

Walking by another window
All alone
Rich women at a lingerie show

They look out and wag their finger
And our fear will always linger
Walking by windows with nowhere to hide

Our content is not known
Their life is always shown
Oh we feel so alone

As Grumpy Old Men dominate;
Control fate in secret meetings to insulate,
While they bait and hate

Their footprints are growing in the air
Above our collective head;
That is why we always feel dread

We want to live before we are dead

VI

In this fallen city, no longer pretty,
Waiting for another election
Natural Selection under their direction

Growing their footprints from the air
We are just a moving dot;
Walking on a scatter plot;

So afraid of getting shot;
They glare at us a lot;
We are young; we are hot; they are not.

We are valued way below gold
We are living in a world that is way too cold
We don’t want to turn into Grumpy Old Men

Like you know who
We want to find someone to love
Someone just like you.

We want to exist
We want to be missed
Sometimes we just need a hug and kiss.

EPICS 2: Spy Included

Crony Capitalism
Secret process
Agenda makes them smile.

Cronies grovel for Winner's affection.
Us, we hide in this demolished section
All alone in this war tone zone.

We are just a moving dot
Walking on a scatter plot
While Grumpy Old Men

Grow their footprints from the air
Why should any of them care
They believe life can't be fair

That is probably why
They seem to always frown
Grumpy Old men always keeping Us down.

We are young so they call us trouble
We hide in the mounting dirt and rubble
In this demolished part of town; bursted bubble.

No one wants to see us around

We know the bulldozers will soon tear up the ground
For the Grumpy Old Men behind a locked door
Are selling contracts to the lowest bidder

Lower than ever before

As their footprints grow in the sky
No one cares if we live or die
We are so lonely, we could cry;

Then we look up into the sky again
We see a promise way above
We know one day there will be love

The Truth is the Lie's only fear
Illusion-making draws many near
Black hair dye and phony smile

Can only last for a little while

But the footprints growing in the sky
Could keep on growing for evermore;
While we are just a moving dot

EPICS 2: Spy Included

Walking all alone on a scatter plot
We are so afraid of getting shot
We are young and our blood is hot

We have nowhere that we are allowed to play
We feel so lost in this decay
But we know there could be a better way

If hate for profit would go away

Crony Capitalism
Secret process
Agenda makes them smile.

Never invited or given a clue
We are so down
We don't know what to do

And we are given nothing to see
For there is no transparency
While Grumpy Old Men

Talk endlessly

While our future waited
For their meeting, so insulated,
To end; we learned to bend; so we could mend

While the trees were taken down
One by one
The Grumpy Old Men did not know

What they had done.
Truth could see
For Truth was living

In every tree.

VII

Body Politics;
Where one still has something to give.
Body Politics;

Depends on who has the right to live.
Body politics
“Still a rich man’s world”

Pre-judgmental
Pride when you are told
That the whole world is your backyard

Inheritance; pull of power;
Civilization; hiding the beast within;
Common sense; inner voice of reason;

Life, water and air;
Simple things
Feed life

Time
Linking the past
Into tomorrow

We are
Grumpy Old Men's
Forgotten sons

Treated like we have an IQ of 12
No one knows where we have been
Or what we have seen.

I heard Truth cry
Not because Truth was afraid to die
But because Truth did not want

To be turned into a lie.

Crony Capitalism
Secret process
Agenda makes them smile.

Body politics
Where you learn to forgive
So the greater good can live

Have space to grow and show
A better way
For Truth could see

For Truth lived in every tree
And every tree
Gave Truth a special view

Of the power of greed;
Depravity;
Stronger force than gravity.

While Grumpy Old Men
Created an illusion
With pseudo-science to cause confusion.

EPICS 2: Spy Included

Black hair dye
And phony smile
That could only last a little while.

Body Politic
Illusion; Evil trick;
Poisoned air; we got so sick.

Truth is their only fear
For Truth shows the way
And was living in every Tree

So Truth could never die
For it had a bird's eye view
Of humanity

As depravity grew in strength
Depravity
Stronger than gravity

Mind of Pretense
Lacking common sense
Pretense; Loving and kind;

A promised spirit that never shows.

VIII

We wait and wait
Until today turns into tomorrow
Without love, there was so much sorrow.

In a world never our own.
We hide feelings that only fools have shown
Lost in the 'no go' section

We are told this is the way
Of natural Selection;
Body Politic; an Evil Trick;

Manufactured consent
Not caring about our content
Telling us to repent

That we have no money for rent.

Behind the darkest walls,
Still standing
In this forgotten town.

As we roam
Without a home
We steal

EPICS 2: Spy Included

A glimpse of humanity
Lost in all this rush
To pave the country side

Nowhere for Trees to hide
And Truth knew
For each tree gave Truth

A special view
Of humanity and depravity
Depravity; a force stronger than gravity.

We stay elastic;
For the Overlord cause so much static
As they turn our world into plastic.

Now there is nowhere to hide
For the fence keeps all the nature in
And we, called the dispossessed, out.

The rush takes over the land
No one has time to take a stand
For they all have faith in the invisible hand.

The cycle of boom and bust

Leads to our demolished part of town
Crumbling in rust
Some get trapped in artificial lust

And some say God was there to trust
For it was written all over their money
They treasured more than life itself.

The trees were taken down
One by one
During that time.

The rains began
Nowhere for the water to soak
The floods took over our part of town.

A power no one could control
Not even with a gun
So the guns were pointed at Us.

Crony Capitalism
Secret process
Agenda makes them smile.

EPICS 2: Spy Included

As Skulls and bones
Are hidden
Under the ground.

And we never made a fuss.
While the Grumpy Old Men
Sat around
On their make-pretend throne

There was still some space
Which could never be owned
Where life could still thrive

Beyond the rush of nine to five.

There was always hope
My Momma said to me
As she held my hand tight

The night she died
She said to me
Always keep your elasticity

And if you hold me for a little bit longer
I know that I will soon grow stronger
As the night sky turns red

Many dread
Knowing what cannot be known
Secret meetings, who knows who will show?

Grumpy Old Men, obstruct like walls
Won't be alive for much longer
And will never see

The world with less ice
Once free, the loss will be the price
The unborn will have to pay.

"When you face the world that is not your own
Remember your content
Deep inside you,"

My Momma said.
Noble Citizen; stuck between two Giants
Could get crushed; risk is hushed;

EPICS 2: Spy Included

Don't let them lead you to premature death
Nouveau Gestapo
March two by two

Rigid; Frigid;
As cold as Arctic ice
Fancy words to entice;

Just remember who you are
And survive the night.
Two Giants might is right;

Pulsating light shone where it could
For it was a great power of its own
So alone and misunderstood

When the light shone
Our scars, which had multiplied,
Glared for all to see.

Crony Capitalism
Secret process
Agenda makes them smile.

The Grumpy Old Men wanted it all
For they knew; soon they would no longer exist
So afraid of what they will miss

The light was in the sky
The bright atmosphere
Hidden in the darkness all around

The light could shine
But never brighten the world of fear
Even though the light was near.

We managed to get by
As the trees stood still majestically
All across our land.

That was said to be made for you and me
Owned by the crown
Not worn by the people.

As the sun faded into time
Many looked at Us
As if our existence were a crime

For now we had no home
For it had been demolished
In all this rush

Very few noticed our loss
For money was the boss
And we had none

Or spoke at all
To Us in a civil tone
Yes we were all alone.

We hoped for peace
But the bulldozers came
Anyway

The demolishing continued
Without a warning
As the morning sun arose

The trees were taken down,
One by one,
They did not know what they had done.

They could not scream; they could not dream
Trees were stuffed in the wood chipper
That was over there.

The trees could not bleed
So the ground did not turn red,
Even though those trees were dead.

As the trees were crushed
One by one
They did not know what they had done.

"It was still a rich man's world,"
Or so it seems
Truth cried out loud

Crony Capitalism
Secret process
Agenda makes them smile.

There was no crowd
And no one heard
But the tree was still standing

EPICS 2: Spy Included

Strong and so alive
For centuries
It had survived

And seen
How mean
Ignorance had grown to be

And it was just a tree
And could not speak
About Love and Unity.

Just like Us; not our world;
Not our place
To even show our face.

“Thirty years of triple net and what did I get?”
I heard a ghostly voice ask;
Once a connected place turned into a dead end street;

While the rich kids have time to play
The day away;
The Demolishment had just begun

Crony Capitalism;
Secret process;
Agenda makes them smile.

And the Grumpy Old Men
Were now baiting
Finding new targets for hating

And we stayed elastic
Tried to avoid their static
As they turned our world

Into plastic

The great trees
Had survives wars
And strife; No longer had life.

The Sun stayed hidden
While the heavens cried
So many trees died that day

We tried to look up
And not down
For life was easier to live that way

But all we saw was the ceiling

Crony Capitalism
Secret process
Agenda makes them smile.

And we had to forgive
For they did not know
What they had done.

The Overlord
Told Farmer Dan
To sell

Or he would raise hell

Until Farmer Dan
Begged for mercy
Property values be dammed

Depended on who was not seen
And who was not heard
So most of Us were treated

Bad and made Us sad.

As if we were part of a herd
And smoke filled the skies
On the other side of the hill

As our world turned to the east
It seemed as if the Sun was setting in the west
Behind the trees

All was never what it seems
But we knew soon all that was treasured
Could be lost

Staying unconcerned was best
For now; we had a place to rest
Our heads, and as we lay

We hoped for a better day.

In this world that was never ours
We remained elastic
To avoid the shock so static

The Overlords caused
While turning everything
Into plastic.

One tree escaped and would not let go
And we understood
The tree was so much more

Than just a piece of wood

For we too were being torn from our ground
With very few around
To even know

We are just a moving dot
Walking on a scatter plot
So afraid of getting shot.

And the birds with the majestic wings
Were often occupied
With other things

For survival of the fittest
Became truer than ever before
As the thunder in the sky

Was hard to ignore

We stayed true
To who we were
For our content gave Us strength

And grew deep inside Us.

Not to be hidden behind a locked door;
For we had no door
The same old story from a time before.

If we spoke
Or were seen
We could be baited for we were hated.

So we hide our face, as we roamed from place to place
For our status
Defined who we were now

Would we find Paradise Lost?
The cost?
Weapons molded into plowshares

It would take a lot of love
Not needed in any back room
Where the process of gloom and doom

Is glorified
We knew something important
Had to be revived

EPICS 2: Spy Included

A place where we could still find trees
For shade
To hide from the glare

Of Pre-judgmental culture
Blinded to discrimination;
Against the young and nature.

And those without means
A harsh world
As Crony Capitalism

System of convenience
Takes hold
Value oil and gold

More than water and air
Unconsciously designing fate
Of Hate and waste.

You can't speak to stakeholders beneath;
Now Skulls and bones; Process of exhaustion
And wealth depletion

Before our life began
We shared Rights of Man;
To live in dignity; beyond an economy hidden in a drawer.

While rich men count their stash of cash
Their guarded eye looks out their window
Onto a Public sidewalk; called their backyard.

Slayers;
Social speculators;
Accidents; Professional Degraders;

Decided where obstacles would be placed
Whenever a certain face
Was seen

God knew
Some said
A place between nature and the unknown stream;

Unified less reason to scream;
So many trees had died
Stakeholders; without a voice there is no choice;

But one little tree stood out all alone.

And Truth had a bird's eye view
And could see
From every tree

Greed; Depravity
A force
Stronger than gravity.

And the secret deciders
Could not see outside their door
For they were hiders.

Truth could see
For Truth lived in every tree
And each bird had grown to be

Truth's eye
So Truth had a greater chance to spread
Before being turned into a lie

As Grumpy Old Men
Hid behind a locked door
They used illusion and confusion

Black hair dye and a phony smile
That would only last a while
So the Overlords were in a hurry

To get all they could.

But they could not see the ice
Melting from the Mountain above.
And we all knew

We needed a home; a place to grow love;
We just needed a bit of land; that would be enough;
And we would need nothing more;

Just a small plot, for our roots to cling to.

As the roads took over the land
In places never mapped before
All the decisions were made

Behind a locked door
While Grumpy Old Men
Black hair dye and phony smile

EPICS 2: Spy Included

Used illusion, confusion
And called it fate;
We hoped it would not be too late

As Grumpy Old Men fell asleep; hidden;
Behind a locked door
Now in control of every power meter in the land

Their gain, our pain;
Professional complainers,
In a process that was secret they said for privacy's sake

But Truth could see
That all they did while they hid
Was waiting for their pay-day

And their love for money and the power
To monopolize
Paved their path to glory;

Still fooled by their first mistake
They did not know what they had done
While smoke and mirrors blocked

And magnified the sun.

And Nature’s beauty; a work not yet complete;
Was fenced in
To only be enjoyed by the elite.

This was the new way; once the old way
As the highway needed more lanes
We grew to be elastic

So we could avoid the Overlords static
As they turned our world
Into plastic.

The Overlords said this was best
For all living creatures
Needing to eat and nest.

And Truth cried
For Truth had a bird’s eye view
Could see from every tree

Greed; depravity;
Stronger force than gravity
As the Grumpy Old Men

EPICS 2: Spy Included

Took all they could
Behind a locked door
That led to many more

Created illusion
Pseudo-science and confusion
Behind black hair dye and phony smile

Still, they would only be living for a while
And Truth cried
For truth did not want to be turned into a lie.

As it rained
The rivers began to flow beyond their banks
For the water was living

Everyone knew
That the Overlords
Would sell the water and air too

If they only could.
Us; we were trapped in this cosmic clock;
Where Opportunity never knocks.

The Overlords captured the stream
On paper during a meeting
Behind a locked door

We could only scream or dream
Or begin the search for a better world
While the old way became the new way.

We saw a hammer in the sky
And we knew we weren't alone
For the power of life

Was still everywhere.
We too were stakeholders
Sharing this common ground

Civilization?
A word
To cause sensation.

Divide and conquer
Was the Overlord's way
Just another Fear Tactic

EPICS 2: Spy Included

Sometimes could cause Panic
While the Overlords
Were busy turning our world into plastic.

Our birthright
To live and exist
Was greatly missed

For the old way became the new way
And it was still a rich man's world
Or so it seemed.

Still, we could feel all this wild life
Pulsate through Us
Not yet the chosen ones

Still Earth's
Forgotten sons
Hanging on the best we can.

And one tree stood tall
And watched it all;
Its destiny was to fall.

The passersby gave Us a dirty look
For the beauty in our demolished
Part of town; was gone

And left Us in manufactured slums
Many called Us bums;
For now we had nothing to maintain

And our faces grew scarred with pain.

IX

The big machines dig for oil
Replacing humans with their toil
One task jobs without design

No negotiating
With bionic tone
Fear the mechanical

For you are alone
Don't Search for Paradise lost
For it has been sold

At an undisclosed cost.
Ethical thinking
Good or bad

When the harm cannot be reversed
Humanity has been cursed
By those living in a time

So long ago
Mean spirit lingered on
Above the ground

Skulls and bones lay beneath

X

Superior orders
From above
Don't call it love

As the rain came down in torrents
And could not soak into the ground
And the floods grew; we knew

For the trees and their root systems

Had been demolished
Inside a wood chipper
What took centuries to grow

Was destroyed so quick

We knew our hope
Depended on calm
We froze to avoid feeling our alarm

The spirit roamed in time
Never finding peace
For he was not made that way.

No one to blame
We had to play the game
To live in balance and harmony

On the land
Not just on
A pile of money

XI

We thanked the power we could not understand
For it seemed to have given Us a hand
Even when the demolishers were in command

EPICS 2: Spy Included

For they too needed water and air
Which made the struggle
A little more fair

Since the Overlords had to care

We are so alone
Walking in the War Tone Zone
We are the forgotten sons

Of Grumpy Old Men
Planning it all
Behind a wall

Growing their footprints in the sky.
We are just a moving dot
Walking through a scatter plot

So afraid of getting shot.

The winds came;
More trees broke and fell
We knew we were living

In a man-made hell.
We were able to find someone kind
In the most demolished part of town.

We watched; having no say;
As our world changed before our eyes;
We did what we could;

In the world that was dominated
By Grumpy Old Men who baited,
In secret meetings so insulated

While growing their footprints in the air.

We are just a moving dot
Walking on a scatter plot
So afraid of getting shot.

Our lives on hold; Still not old;
We have passed the test
Of manufactured distress

By overcoming our duress
Staying numb under stress
While Truth lives in every tree

EPICS 2: Spy Included

Watching over you and me;
It had a bird's eye view
Over all Humanity.

While Grumpy Old men dissolve privacy
Wanting control over all Destiny
Denying their threat over democracy;

Grumpy Old Men destined to die
Turned Truth's voice
Into a lie

For Truth was what is and what was,
Evidence behind that locked door,
Hidden so no one knew.

"And without you, sweet birds,
I would be so alone
Hiding in these shadows

Always out of view."

I heard Truth take a breath and continue to say,
"I see Depravity growing all around
Stronger force than gravity holding onto the ground.

Evil in disguise
Hate softens
What should make a person cry.

Greed justifies so much waste
Consuming in too much haste
Transforming destiny

Into a place more hostile
Harder to smile
Or want to linger for a while.

By design
Man-made hell
Needed struggle; don't give up the fight

For what we all knew is right.

There were many ghosts
Lost without a name;
They were not to blame.

Only a voice
Could leave a plea;
So that one day

EPICS 2: Spy Included

We would see
The power of True Love
Growing across this land.

The birds with majestic wings
Needed very little
For they had their own way

And Truth could see
From every tree
And was waiting silently;

To feed; while humans
Were left dying
In all this greed.

For their hands were tied
Behind their back
Planning another attack

Growing their footprints
From the air;
While baiting and hating

We knew we had to stay elastic
To avoid the static
A mind-war fear tactic

While the Overlords
Turned our world into plastic
Bones and skulls below our Earth

Wanted their power back.

And the power hungry
Politician
Told the farmer to give up his land

For farmland spoiled his view
When playing golf
As the ball

Rolled down
An artificially green hill
Just for a thrill

The land was taken out of food production.

The farmer said no
The politician said go
For the farmer was said to be spoiling the view

EPICS 2: Spy Included

"We control the rise and fall
Of property value
Not you,"

The Overlord said.
"You must not be seen
Nor heard

Our power of inheritance
Makes Us who we are"
And Truth cried

Truth could see
Humanity from every tree.
Greed; Depravity;

Stronger Force than Gravity.
As Grumpy Old Men
Hid behind illusion

Black hair dye and confusion.
And unethical legalist said
'Our might is right."

We are behind this locked door
We are safe here; nothing to fear;
As he began to memorize rule after rule,

Victimizing Us with his projection.

Truth began to cry
Didn't want to be turned
Into another lie.

And Truth had a bird's eye view;
For Truth could see
From every tree.

And knew
The old way was not new
Unethical Legalist; just another fool;

Still a rich man's world; So cruel;
Mind of Pretense; lacking common sense;
Truth could see and cried

Did not want to be turned
Into a lie
While watching every tree die.

XII

We knew the game
We had to play
For the Overlords had nothing new to say.

We stayed elastic
To avoid the static
While the Overlord turned everything into plastic.

The birds with majestic wings
Helped Us think of noble things
Though some were caught in the fences

That were all around
Many were able to fly away
Giving Us strength

To face a new day

The birds with majestic wings
Saw what could never be spoken
While our pain had been awoken.

Our privacy
Our boundaries
Everything we knew

Was under vicious attack
By the baiters, the haters
And the property value inflators

Planned behind closed doors
For the truth
Would take years to show.

Us; the young were still elastic.
More able to recover from the Overlord's static;
While they turned our world into plastic.

Once truth grew visible, the Overlords
Would no longer exist nor be
Still we would never be free

For the Overlords would remain in memory

Paying the debt was always delayed
Waiting for the day the Overlords would fade way
Into the past.

And their debt would be left behind
For Us to repay
For we were the generation born into doom

And often we forgot the flowers that bloom
Freely
In this world of gloom

We followed the sign
Promising to see
The best place in the world

But that place could no longer be
For the Tree of Unity
Had gone missing.

XIII

We searched anyway
For we all agreed
That Paradise lost must be found

So we searched for that place
Promised to Us
A long time ago

While rich men count their cash
In front of their window
No common sense is needed

Hiding the beast within; Snobocrat;
The new aristocrat
They will hate you, if they hate your hat.

Some have guns
Not knowing creates
A state of runs.

We looked on the ground
For tracks; a path to follow;
Which may lead Us to our Promised Land.

It was said to be

A place of peace and love
Sheltered by mountains on all sides
A place where we would all belong

We followed the Path
And to our dismay
We found what we were looking for

Blocking our way

EPICS 2: Spy Included

The Tree of Unity had taken root;
And was sharing our air;
So we made the rule

To never be a tool for a fool
Or let our Tree of Unity be sold
For paper or gold.

In a land of boom and bust
Everything we knew had turned to rust
Except our love, except our trust;

We hugged Tree of Unity
And then each other.
We called our neighbors

Sister and Brother.
And as we held hands
We felt a glow beginning to flow;

No more excuses to discriminate
And agitate;
Or poison the world with hate.

Across foreign lands
We watched as the Overlords
Dropped their guns.

And a new era had begun;
And what a wonderful world
It was.

THE END

FLIGHT

#23. FLIGHT

I

Breaking sound barrier; what a show
Money burning
In the air

Prestige
On display
Praise to the War Machine

That you don't see every day.
Some machines spy
Others fly; breaking the speed of sound.

Pointy nose;
Heavy; aiming for the ground
Trigger Words; Fibber Words

Super Sonic Boom;
Shock Waves left behind
As Beautiful War Machine breaks the speed of sound;

We heard thunder as we stood on the ground;
A cold shiver made us tremble in fear.
"Fear feeds paranoia and takes control."

A ghost called Joe said to a ghost called Bill.

"Our Beautiful War Machine does more than just kill
It gives everyone
A thrill,"

Joe Replied, wishing that he had not died.

"The War Machine's role is to keep us in control;
When we were human we had nothing
But praise for the cosmic disturbance."

Bill the ghost sighed as he knocked on Heaven's Door.

Heaven; a Place
Humans cannot know
For it is said; they have never been there before.

II

Only lack of fuel can slow
The Beautiful War Machine
As it breaks the sound barrier

Flying Inquisitor
Searching out for
The Unwanted Visitor.

Flying Inquisitor
Takes flight and hurries out of sight;
Shiny dot in the sky

Shrinking the vastness of our Airspace
Designed to fit
The Flying Inquisitor's orders

Urgency to find the spot
And to drop
Payload after the Cosmic Boom.

Feels like thunder on the ground
This is not the sound of Secret Love
Penetrating into the sky above

This is a world turned upside down
Where the Glass Ceiling
Becomes the floor

EPICS 2: Spy Included

And we try to hold on to what we had before.

When Secret Love grew unconditionally
When wealth was divided
And multiplied freely

Frozen moment in time
Secret Love which kept hope alive
Refusing to be alienated nor baited.

Hoping to find the secret
We are not meant
To know

For that secret door
Was said to be forbidden
To humans; for evermore

As the Flying Inquisitor
Turned our world upside down
The Glass Ceiling became the floor

While we held on to what we had before.

A world; not ours to know any more.
We are the prey
Of the Flying Inquisitor

We wait for our darkest hour
Hoping that the secret door
Will be open to us that day.

It is said that the secret door
Is not yours nor mine
Nor owned by the Flying Inquisitor

Still the Flying Inquisitor
Can turn the world
Upside down

Where the Glass Ceiling
Becomes the floor
And we try to hold on to what we had before

As we try
To find the key;
To the secret door

EPICS 2: Spy Included

Lies in one's Soul-head
Bill the Ghost said to Joe the ghost
Remembering how the steel nose

Pulled him down too fast;

We all hear each other's fear
After the Sonic Boom
Brings some joy; other's gloom.

Moisture in the air; forming into water droplets
Clouds grow;
Nature's Way;

The Supersonic Eye
Sees all; heavy nose knows;
Justice is blind

Not easily defined
Behind the curtain of protocol;
Amidst the thunder; Nature's call;

King of Vitriol
Blamed us all
When the cake could not rise

He told us we could eat the flat cake
Anyway
And then wished us a good day

The Flying Inquisitor
Targets
Dehumanized prey

Harming those that get in between;
The scene is mean
But the Flying Inquisitor

Cannot be seen
By men with less
Than Men of Fortune

Angry tone
Targeting those all alone
Men of Fortune; cold as stone

Turning our world upside down
Glass Ceiling becomes the floor
While we hang on to what we had before.

EPICS 2: Spy Included

Men of Fortune
Fondle their weapons of choice
To lord over the Broken Hearted;

Men of Fortune
So brave behind their Beautiful War Machines
They only share Secret Love when they whisper

Coward; they target those alone
Can't be called a crime
For their self-appointed authority

Lifts them above it all
So they can watch
Those beneath crawl

In the upside down world
Where the Glass Ceiling
Becomes the floor

Not much left
They have it all
Men of Fortune; Men of History;

Men fondling their weapons while causing misery
Too numb;
The weary people bow their heads.

While Men of Fortune
Roam inside places
Blown off the map

Steely gate
Without a key
Surrounds those who hunger to be free;

Forced to live a life of pain and sorrow
So afraid of Tomorrow;
Men with Machine Nose in the air

Too heavy; Gravity pulls Machine Nose down to Earth.

Now pointing to the ground;
Machine Nose points up into the air;
Again.

Travels faster than sound;
Thunder cracks by our feet on the ground;
Lost time; condensed space;

EPICS 2: Spy Included

Just another face
Ageing behind a frown
Anger once the tool now the foe;

Creating a scene
Hoping the foe will lose control
And then they will fly away

Into their world
That they own everyday
While hanging on

The fool forgets about tomorrow
Shock waves
Created as steel nose

Grows too heavy
And must come down
For it takes a lot of fuel

To travel against gravity
Just another Force at work
Treating those below

As if they were a jerk.
Must know your own mind;
Beyond skin;

Never letting outside in.

Callous Man
Sees too much misery
Can no longer be kind;

Why would he let outside in?
Pride which arrogates the willfully blind;
Above our heads; so high we cannot see;

I hear the sonic roar
Breaking the sound barrier; can't be ignored
Even though it can't be seen

The pride which it is arrogating
Is mean, overseen by no one;
Spinning around in the air

The mighty feeling
Faster than sound
Sometimes breaks the windows on the ground.

EPICS 2: Spy Included

Freedom to arrogate power
Too much might
From the air

Brings down steely nose
No balance;
Pulled into Gravity's glance.

"We fly in this immense sky
We see nothing but emptiness
Looming in the Horizon every day

We must fly for it is the only life we know,"
Bill the ghost said to Joe the ghost
"Now if we could only see

What lies on the other side
Of Heaven's Door," Joe replied.
Could be peace we were looking for

Before we died."

And I knew Peace
Was just a promise
Waiting for us; at Heaven's Door.

Emptiness in the horizon; shrunk
By super-sonic flight
The roaring thunder in the night

Gentle world
Somewhere above
Is said to exist

So easy to miss
We heard a crack on the ground
We knew the meaning of the sound

Sonic Boom had brought gloom
To many who now felt doom
And Might be frozen in hate

Micromanagement; mismanagement;
Disengaged from the pain
Targeted for harsher rules

We dodge Smirking Fools

The enemy described in the script
The enemy that we never meet
The enemy that will never admit defeat.

EPICS 2: Spy Included

Enemy competes with the boss
Enemy who contributes to our loss
The enemy is more like us

Than we will ever know.

The enemy of the master mind
Competes for the wealth all around
In the vast world shrunk by sonic flight

Flying in the middle of the night
Showing might
While the master-mind calls this right

The Flying Inquisitor
Looking for the Uninvited Visitor
Who knows Freedom is just in the mind

As he roams into the Negative Zone
He never felt so alone
For the people there have hearts of stone

Micromanaged; mismanaged;
Targets are hidden in System Code;
Sonic Boom; success for some;

For others life grows into gloom and doom.

Wasteland way too soon.
Emptiness
Inside Out

The Flying Inquisitor
Turning the world upside down
Glass Ceiling becomes the floor

We hang on to everything that we had before.

As the Mass Mind closed
The Mass Mind became smaller
Trapped in tunnel vision

No expected objectivity in their decision.

III

"How can we be civilized?
In such a barbaric world?"
I wondered to myself

As Impulsive Noise
Adjusted to our manufactured consent
Our voice could not be heard; unknown was our Content.

EPICS 2: Spy Included

A fact; an assumption or an act
No one knows what is true
Anymore.

No channel of communication
When we needed it the most
Cold air surrounded us

And some said ghosts from a lost time
Were drawing near
Ghosts who wrote rules a long time ago;

To disrupt the flow
Of thought; decay turned to rot
And overruled any discussion

The Inquisitor was paid to win the argument;
"First one through the wall
Will be the first one to fall,"

I heard a ghostly voice complain
I was surrounded by cold air
One more time again.

Unwritten protocol;
The masters' call;
Too sad to walk tall;

Protocol;
Unwritten policy
Followed before Tea.

A fact; an assumption or an act
No one knows what is true
Anymore.

IV

Vast sky
An ancient world's Ceiling
Lost in the cold; unappealing;

Flight Path;
Wildlife scatters out of the way
Super Sonic Might

A fright
For birds in flight
Looking for worms

Hiding beneath the light
Of day
Nature's way

EPICS 2: Spy Included

In the night
A watcher said,
"Watch out for predators dear.

They are near those who walk.
They will pretend to want to talk
And you will be too tired to fight

A hard line that we must repeat
Never admit defeat
Only the chosen few would ever be elite

Fewer could afford to eat
Starvation became hidden
Truth became forbidden

For time is ticking away the day
Weakening Strength; Lost Might;
If caught you will die in fright."

We could hear the Flying Inquisitor
Overhead
Turning our world upside down

What was once the Glass Ceiling
Was now a floor
As we hung on to everything that we had before.

In the land which could not innovate
Many were controlled in feelings of hate
And could never be free.

It was now the middle of the night
I knew that I must take refuge
And find

A tree that I could hide behind
And stay until the morning light
Could shine

I didn't need the tree to be mine
For the tree I found was free
Basking in the peace of Nature's Equity

The soul of Equity
Divides and multiplies freely;
From the Creation's heart.

EPICS 2: Spy Included

Tree was still standing that night
But fell before the morning light
The Flying Inquisitor

Was still in flight.

To anyone that was not their kind
Many became willfully blind
To their cruelty

Which destroyed Equity
While we tried to blend
Into the ground

Without getting buried there
We still had a lot to share
And believed Equity would re-balance

One day soon
Equity would touch this Valley of Doom
If we kept an open mind

The machines took the jobs
And the brown shirts were used to
Blending individuals into mobs

They were picked for size
Often despised
Pride allowed them to stare

As if I wasn't there
I was too young to have lost my dream
As barriers went up to create a new revenue stream

We are waiting until the debt bubble pops
The brown shirts are wanna be cops
Disengaged and micro-managed;

They did not know what could have been
There was not much that they had ever seen
Chaos was disguised

In Stereotypes and hype
To devalue Content
So Fools could rule.

We knew

The Inquisition was in full swing
The Cosmic Boom
Would made our ears ring

EPICS 2: Spy Included

Even though we hoped

The human part of the Inquisitor
Would give us something to salvage
He had grown too savage

And was turning the world upside down
The Glass Ceiling became the floor
While we hung on to all we had before.

The Inquisition
Destruction of Competition
The new Bigotry

Hard to see
Was a state of mind
Made some willfully blind

But the Tree was still standing
Symbol of Equity
Nature's Way

As the darkness of the night
Created invisibility
Only the moon shone nearby;

While I found myself alone
Waking up underneath
A fallen tree

With bird poop all over me

I had a piece of bread
Which I shared
With the birds that were not dead

They shared a song with me
Which lingered in in my head
Promising a better day

Bringing on a new way
Once the night of horror had faded
Leaving my part of town in a pile of rubble.

The Inquisition's smoke
Blocked the sun
No apology needed; damage could not be undone.

I raised my eyes to the sky; above
All this trouble
And I knew it would take

EPICS 2: Spy Included

A lot of love
To turn this Inquisition around
For his toxic state of hate

Was soaking into our ground
With a crack,
We heard the Sonic Boom from the air

And we knew
Many more would be
Frozen in hate

Could only sustain
The Negative Zone's Fate
The Inquisition had blocked out the sun

Wasteland
Emptiness
Inside Out

As the Mass Mind closed
It became smaller
Trapped in tunnel vision

No objectivity in their decision.

As conditions were left to deteriorate
Decay ate until there was nothing there
No one left to care

And we the people knew
If we didn't find a new way soon
It would be too late.

We did not respond to the brown shirts
While they tried to stir up anger
We kept our eyes on our friends above

For they flew closest to Heaven's door
Which one day would open
For those pure enough

Submerged in Secret Love

We strengthened our selves
Refusing to be warehoused on shelves
We waited for the light to burst into the sky

For the new day
Promised a better way;
Giving us time to find the key

To the secret door

Somewhere up above
A place where there still was love
Once freed would fill the sky

And tumble down upon us
Still standing
On this scorch

Wasteland
Emptiness
Inside Out

Hoping with all our might that the secret

Would reveal itself to us
And turn our pain into might
We gazed into the sky again

And we could see what the light could do
Made us cover our eyes; it was day
And the sun was too bright

We felt the light's might
And hoped that there was a force
Watching over us.

The King of Vitriol's rule had begun
The Negative Zone's Fate
Was in his hands

Earth's Equity
Was growing in Her Tree
Nature's Way

As we continued on
We knew every path was being watched
A supersonic bullet overhead

Left Wasteland
And Emptiness
As we looked from Inside Out.

The note on the wall said
All bags must be left
At the door.

THE END

EQUITY LOST

#24. EQUITY LOST

I

Janis dressed for success
Walked by those who were dispossessed
Ignored those who would oppress

She built value through time.
Empowered;
She knew what was hers and what was mine.

She walked down the street
Lined with patio chairs;
Where many dined on lobster;

Many were owned by the Monster Mobster.

What was; sometime yesterday;
Will now fade away.
For today is a new day

The order of things
Beyond the upside down world
That could turn the glass ceiling into a floor

EPICS 2: Spy Included

Safety net was gone
Angry Boys just like dots
Moving around on scatter plots

Janis hoped for a better life;
With her beau; even though
Monster Mobster

Held on to the Ghostly Boys; would not let them go.
So hurt inside
They wanted to hurt back somehow

Widening the Negative Zone
Where backpacks and everything they owned
Must be left at the door

Like getting kicked; felt so atrocious;
While they laughed; had to survive
Many became ferocious.

Obstruction everywhere; Ghostly Angry Boys
Lived in a world where no one could care
Broken spirits for evermore

No opening for engagement
Skateboards slamming
Into another door

Direction not so clear
Turning east they see
A steely beast

Turning west
They see the sea
Some say a doorway to Eternity

So how can it be
Necessary
To micromanage

Until their heart was broken
Life was never nothing at all
A long time ago

Life of quality
Depended on location of Equity.
What side are you on?

Behind the wall;
The winning side
Needs a losing side

No vision
When making a decision
Needed.

EPICS 2: Spy Included

The micromanagers with guns
Were on watch all night
No one felt safe

Though we were told the process was right;
Would keep us safe;
Some felt too stifled and weak to speak.

The wall could not confine
Value
For it had a life of its own

As currency value paralleled oil
Prices in the bubble could only be inflated
Only machines were needed to toil

Before they became outdated
And what we said
Meant nothing at all

For we all were on the wrong side of the wall.

They had no words to speak
So the guns gave them might
While blood flowed

In us all night
Made us glad
To still be alive

Though we were told we were
Living in a world
Where goodness could not exist

And where we would never be missed;
As the youth were ran out of town;
The remaining few were always put down.

"My friends mean a lot
To me; too bad they were treated so bad,"
Janis almost said but left the thought inside her head.

The old felt the loss
And wondered why they were still so cross
While the future was being forced out of the door

The youth's world was turned upside down
The Glass Ceiling
Became the floor

EPICS 2: Spy Included

Some of the youth hid under that floor
While the Monster Mobster laughed
As the old hid behind their fence of wire

Monster Mobster knew
Their fear
Would never tire.

And the old
Felt no sorrow
When the loss of their town's tomorrow

Was being pushed away
Not allowed to stay
Could not come back another day.

Now transient
The youth
Were only allowed a short stay

Though the cost of emergency shelter
Was more
Than a real home

Many went missing
And were under the ground.
They could not be found;

They made no sound;

The Monster Mobster
Kept on killing
For it was thrilling

And Janis knew
What it was like
To have nothing left to lose.

They held on to their energy
Within a rigid force
Frigid heart so cold

It got that way
As they grew old
Piling up their gold

Putting everyone down,
Always wearing a frown;
Whatever they did took too long.

EPICS 2: Spy Included

They could not feel strong
For they were too tired
Confined behind their fence so wired.

During the time of yesterday
They had some things they desired
Hoping it would make them more admired

They had no clue
What would transpire
Behind that fence made of wire.

The Monster Mobster knew

When their pain had awoken
It would go unspoken
Even though they felt so broken.

The Monster Mobster took over the mind;
The Force was steely and very unkind
Made many willfully blind.

Scary city;
Used to be pretty;
Though there was no sorrow

When they locked out their tomorrow.
They needed no vision
To make a decision

For random luck
Was good enough
During the years gone by.

And the Dark Force was everywhere
Didn't care; treated everyone the same;
Even though the Dark Force didn't have a name.

For many; only escape was in drink;
Getting lost in the crowd;
When they awoke

The Ghostly Angry Boys
Were covered in ink
Still trapped in the poorest part of town

With no way out.

EPICS 2: Spy Included

Called dangerous
Framed within
Self-fulfilling prophecies

Went on breaking
The heart
Before its awakening.

Their heartbeat was flattened
But not yet dead;
Heart had less intensity

To see the ever changing sky turn red.
One would have to ask why
Tomorrow was left forgotten.

And the ghosts of yesterday
Were flying in the wind;
We closed the window

And every curtain;
But the pain
Would still linger

Waiting to pound again.

Lost in the growing city
Rural fringe and all its Equity
Left hidden behind the fence of wire.

Give and take;
Anything less
A big mistake.

Equity;
What you learn
What you earn

What you return.

Steely Grandma watched
As Ghostly Angry Boys
Slammed their skateboards into glass.

In the Upside Down World

Monster Mobster was in charge of the Negative Zone
Where backpacks and everything you owned
Must be left outside the door;

EPICS 2: Spy Included

It felt so atrocious;
To survive
One became ferocious.

Process of becoming transient
Was shadowed
Behind the new concrete and glitter.

And only a few felt sorrow
As they locked out their tomorrow
While counting their surplus

Of a little over a billion.
The pool contributors were 35 million;
Less than sixty dollars each;

They had nothing more to teach
And the future was out of reach.
For the transient walking in the halls

Between razor walls
Death; the other side of life.
Breath; you must take one

Even during times of strife.

Reality reflects
In the mirror of doom
And growing gloom;

In the poor part of town;
Just another Negative Zone.
Ghostly Angry Boys pick on those alone

Ghostly Angry Boys
With Steely Grandma
Who does not speak

But just drives them around
While the missing
Are sometimes under the ground

Never to be found
For they do not make a sound
They left their broken bodies

Behind; in a world where they were despised;

EPICS 2: Spy Included

Never saying a word
As Ghostly Angry Boys
Slam their boards again;

Someone's Equity
In the Negative Zone
Had just been degraded

Couldn't sooth their pain
So Micromanaged
They did not know what to do

When their chain
Had been loosened
Had no principles

Just strange rituals
Made them feel
Like individuals.

II

Beautiful child
New to this world
There is so much he needs to know

Every day he will grow
Into a new tomorrow
There will be some sorrow

When he finds
Not everything thrown to the floor
Will bounce back up

Elasticity
By design
Up and down

Dead Cat in the hat
Bouncing off the wall
Before the fall.

Beautiful child
So new to this world
One day when he is old

He will have been told
To see nothing; hear nothing;
And serve with a smile

For he will only be here for a little while.

There will be lost years;
Trying to prove a negative
Time; well he would never have enough;

Even if the world managed;
To grow more love.
Trying to prove a negative

Would leave his psyche damaged;
Hurting too bad to smile
During his profile.

Which would try to define
A free spirit
Within a hard line.

Stay for only a short time;
Any longer it will be treated like a crime;
Hell; living in a world where you never belong.

III

Today is the day to take action
Can one fight evil to transform it
Or does fighting evil require evil deeds?

Bobby's son asked his father;
Who could not reply;
Felt dismay;

Did not know what to say;
"We all need someone to feed
Dying in all this greed,"

The father said as a reply
He did not want to lie;
Did not want his son to cry.

"So when you fight evil so atrocious;
To survive
One becomes ferocious."

"How do you know
If you are going to win?"
The son asked his dad

Hoping to not make him mad.
"I suppose you will never know"
As boy's dad remembered Ghostly Angry Boys

EPICS 2: Spy Included

From a time, long ago.

"You might not survive
You could be buried alive
But the cause will never die

The cause will just grow
As it feeds from today's sorrow
Into tomorrow

And create a system
More brutal than he;
The one who will never see.

Manipulation through loss
Heartache grows into power
Becomes the boss."

The dad said as a reply
He did not want to lie
Did not want his son to cry.

"And this war will end all wars
That is what we are fighting for
A war to end all wars."

So atrocious;
To survive
One becomes ferocious.

The father added.
Sometimes though
If we see good in others

Our love can grow
So we become
Universal sisters and brothers.

After we see atrocity
It is harder
To be so free.

IV

"Modern War Machines
Costs how many houses?
How many trains?"

No one asked why
As they bowed down
To Carrot-stick god

And his War Machine.

Flown by a clone;
Wing man was a drone.
We were lost in this crowd

Felt so alone

Our minds no longer free;
First to go
Was Curiosity.

Many bowed down to Slander and Tyranny
Defining an enemy
Calmed the need to fear

Cultural conditioning
Economic Warfare
Where no one was rich enough

And where many despised the poor.
Cold faced;
She slammed the door;

Before anyone could ask for more.

And then she said,
"I don't need anyone to feed,
It is not my fault

They are dying in all this greed.
I am just influenced
By what I need.

It may seem atrocious;
To survive
One becomes ferocious.

V

Bow down
Show reverence
To your Carrot-stick god

Or drown
In the sea of blood
Now that the angel has emptied

His Bowl

EPICS 2: Spy Included

To soothe his conscience
Neighbors will call him pious
No one will notice his bias

The numerator is zero
The denominator is zero
You get nothing from nothing

Rigid
One rule fits all
Before the fall

Leaves of color
Are still green
And the sun shines in our hair.

Lost elasticity
Diminished Equity
Loss of entitlement and citizenship

Zero was on top of Zero;
And nothing was made from nothing;
No longer a person of means;

For Equity was no longer seen alive in dreams.
Equity; more than just capital saved over the years;
Equity was about fairness in a world with so many tears.

As nothing from nothing grows.
The Crony Capitalist knows
The right people

While war machines delegate
Who to hate
Who to kill.

What a thrill;
To watch the machines
Fly inside the air

One way and wrong way
One dimensional
Is so intentional

Not really conventional
For innovation
Just is; without authorization

What didn't exist does now;
Without Documentation;
Just needed Consideration.

While refugees from the War Tone Zone
Know we can't care
And life is just not fair.

VI

Ghosts arrived in a swarm
Left their broken bodies behind
In a cold world often unkind

Fences of wire
Could never inspire
Left nothing to admire

The wind blew off a hat
The boy missed the bus
Before it turned

Exploded and burned
Unexpected;
Could not be predicted.

The losses were many
In the Divided City
Immortality

Was their only hope.

Modern War Machines
Fueled with dead matter and hard lines
Sometimes could not kill beyond the skin.

Many ran
Into a new life
So they could live new dreams

Forget the screams

As they followed
Living streams
Hope was kept alive

Only way to survive
As we; all refugees; of some sort;
Felt the sun

Shining on our hair.

EPICS 2: Spy Included

Almost a prison land
Behind Mega Walls
And deleted border towns

The new Deceiver
Looked like a clown
With his upside down frown

To match the upside down world
Glass ceiling now a floor
Creating alienation throughout the nation.

Hate turned vibes into brick
Hate made many sick
Angry Ghostly Boys looking for someone to pick

A fight with; baiters and haters;

Only power they knew
Was making others crawl.
Otherwise they did nothing at all;

For Equity was no longer in dreams
And no one cared
Even though Equity was more

Than capital saved over the years
In a world
With way too many tears.

No one asked why
As they bowed down
To the Carrot-stick god

And His War Machine.

Flown by a clone;
Wing man was a drone.
We were lost in this crowd

And Janis felt so alone.

We all knew
More than ever before
Inequity was Tyranny's atrocity;

Made many look so atrocious.
And in order to survive
Many became ferocious.

It would take courage
To grow enough Goodwill and Love
To give Peace a chance.

THE END

DEATH RATTLE

#25. DEATH RATTLE

I

How brave were we;
Never questioned those above;
Steely eyed;

Now lying in this field;
With no color at all;
For this was last call.

The battle cry
We heard
Moved us

Like a herd
Too fierce
To be called sheep

Now so many lie here
Gasping for breath
While drowning in death.

We are just living cells;
Dying one by one;
Dying before life has really begun.

Our side has a Holy Book
Their side has a Holy Book
And we had no time to look

Inside either book
For ourselves
And now we never will.

II

So ready were we for battle;
But nothing prepared us well
For the Death Rattle Hell.

We heard each other's chilling Rattle all around;
As we were lying on the ground.
We expected Heaven's Door

To open; and nothing more.

Our eyes were focused on the sky
And wondered why all we could hear
Was each other's after battle Death Rattle.

We stared at the sky anyway
While the birds flew all around
Their song could not drown

Death Rattle's chilling sound.
There was no Angel's Welcome
Though it might yet come.

We heard
Trumpets blaring
But they were only our own.

We had thirst but could not drink
We were drowning in death
And struggling for breath.

It was hard to say what we missed the most
As we were becoming part of our Living Host.
We could not tell the fully living

What they needed to know; what we know now;
If we had only been more loving and giving
We would have all reached a higher standard of living.

It was not too late for the fully living below;
To change the Mastermind so it could grow kind
And less greedy and willfully blind

For us; all chance was gone.

As we were flowing into the other side
We tried to forget
What we could only regret.

III

We were expecting an open door
To a place better than we ever had before
But what we found was not as merry

As the place that we left behind.
We expected angels with wings
Singing in harmony

But we were met by birds of every Earthly kind;

Our bodies were broken
Beyond repair
But part of our minds

Went on living
And joined heaven's light;
Free from Negativity's plight;

Free from need;
No longer enslaved
In the Mastermind's greed.

IV

The Cold on the other side
Brought chills to the living too;
Shared thrills with those who knew

That we had returned
To our living Host
Earth and Sky

Never asking why
We were too ready to die
Before we really lived.

THE END

FEAR

#26. FEAR

I

So alone
In the Negative Zone
Fearing those they do not know

Cramped in the city
Squashed together.
No room to breathe.

Fear;
We feel it
Year after year.

We know the cost;
Tear after tear.
We don't know how to count what is lost.

Beautiful Child
Depends on love
And a gentle touch.

Close your eyes now
For War Time is on Parade;
To win one must know how to degrade.

EPICS 2: Spy Included

I see the hope in your eyes;
Beautiful Child;
What will this fog of war leave behind for you?

And no war is holier than your innocence.
Oh Beautiful Child
What will be left for you?

Small town one percent
Never caring about informed consent
As long as they can gouge you in your rent.

II

Oh Beautiful Child
What shall we keep
Your destiny is shaped while you sleep.

Subtle fear of loss can grow violent in the mind;
Can make many unkind;
So willing to be willfully blind.

Oh Beautiful Child, you have no past to leave behind;
While the weapons of war degrade
Seem to always be on parade.

Mis-leaders attached to opposing books
They are always quick to judge those
On looks.

They pray to the thing;
They hope for the thing;
They fight for the thing.

And once the battle is won;
The thing rusts and fades away;
Never able to stay for another day.

Timocracy;
Descendants of a noble aristocracy;
Froze social mobility;

So long ago.
No turning point;
No entry point;

Very few would know;
Out of sight
Was out of mind

Inferior nature
Of Timocrats
Made it so.

Social Power
Deriving from wealth
A long time ago.

Monetized matter too.

But below the ground
Invisible forces were raging
The Timocrats were too narrow minded

To see
For they were only descendants
Of a noble aristocracy.

Timocrats
Born into wealth
Which gave them power

From birth
This is how
They valued their worth.

Negative Social Reproduction
Closed doors
Of schools

Fools
Hoped
To rule fools.

The one percent and their wanna bees
Swarm around their chosen one.
See how they hate

While shaping her fate;
Too hardened to change their minds.
Now for Louise it is too late.

The deed has been done;
They group like beasts
As they mark their feast.

Negative Social Reproduction
Frozen in Time
No turning point; no entry point;

EPICS 2: Spy Included

Steely rigid Timocrats;
So top heavy;
Could not move forward;

Descendants of a noble aristocracy
Never needing to grow
Never needing to know

The other side of the universe.
Timeless forces
Earth, Water and Fire;

Sky power;
Electrifying;
Terrifying;

The source of Nature's force
They could never see;
They could never be;

Even if they wanted to.
Too much fright
Paralyzed what could have been might.

The Timocracy
Were fools
Needing fools to rule.

Oh see Fear entice;
See Fear pretending to be nice;
See Fear and its cost;

Innocence is now lost.

See Fear in their face;
See Fear all over the place.
In this world too afraid to love.

Big bucks to be made
In war and gloom,
Love is free and there is never enough.

Love knows that Peace
Could never come too soon
In this land of gloom and doom.

So many turn away
Not knowing what to say
While the Beautiful Child

Has nowhere to play.
The world is on the brink
Of war; some are driven to drink;

Others don't know what to think.

III

Oh how Louise grew
Until she could not fit
Into the pigeon hole

Anymore;
All the gatekeepers made sure
That the door was always closed to her;

Unless she paid a professional assessor
$1.5 K
To stay

Connected
And to be educated
To a higher degree;

Otherwise
She would have no
Opportunity;

Accept drinks that were free.
Days were buried into the past
Rather fast.

She could not find a place she could afford to keep;
So she had nowhere to sleep;
While every door was being slammed in her face.

There was nowhere she could belong;
Not one single place
To call her own. Louise was all alone.

IV

There was a place
Across the sea
And far away

Where we were told the war was about Liberty;
We were told what to fear and what to kill.
We were not shown the blood and gore,

EPICS 2: Spy Included

Though we had heard about it all before,
We didn't know what we were fighting for.
Very few could listen;

And very few could see;
The rarest freedom of all
Is to be the best you can be.

Sharing the same host
A planet so blue
We were all brothers and sisters

And life was our glue.
We were stuck together
In a system of unity

That we could not see
And the greatest freedom of all
Was to stay real during the Fall.

To never be defined;
Defiled;
Captured by negativity's pull;

And lost in Eternity's Wind.

The war was very far away across the sea;
We were told
That we must fight for Liberty.

And Big Brother told us who was mentally ill;
And who to fear;
Who to shun when they were near.

Oh Beautiful Child
Still so small
Living behind the wall

He shows so much love.
He feeds on love.
He becomes that love.

V

Oh the lead man
How he could plan.
And he knew

That he could unite
And delight
After the Demise of Louise;

EPICS 2: Spy Included

She would not recover from her latest fright;
Which lasted all night;
Everyone said that it wasn't right;

But the villain was let go
And was no longer in sight.
He had tasted blood

And felt his might
Now the little man
Felt like a big man.

Dirty Politics; Shitily Managed;
Win any way you can
Makes a little man feel like a big man.

Let him smirk
While he jerks
Going to work.

Defame;
Slander her name;
Manufacture consent;

Pretend that you are a member
Of the one percent;
Entitled to bring anyone down;

Blank face now wearing a frown.

To shape intent so criminal
Into something appearing more civil;
So a little man can feel like a big man.

How did Hitler Rise?
Was he living
Behind a disguise?

While he generated Fear
And absolute control
How could he have been like that?

What hurt him so bad?
What made him so mad?
Imagine what could have been

EPICS 2: Spy Included

If peace had been given the chance
It needed to grow
From today into tomorrow.

Timocrat could not be criticized;
He was just a little man
Wanting to feel like a big man.

Dirty Politics; Shitily Managed;

He will need someone even smaller
To shout at;
Dirty Politics; Shitily Managed;

Get what you can;
So the little man
Can feel like a big man.

Big brother announced her name;
Helped to degrade the woman behind the door;
So that attacking her became fair game;

Less than criminal now;
For everyone said
That they knew all about her;

Though they never knew her at all
For she was living behind
A make-shift wall.

And the evil tone;
Echoed through the Negative Zone.
When Louise was all alone.

Big Brother was watching
Through the eye
In the sky.

He didn't shed a tear
He didn't cry
He began to believe the lie.

Now it was said all knew her;
And the little man who wanted to be a big man
Never questioned the lie

EPICS 2: Spy Included

Even when his cruelty made her cry
And made him a lesser man
Than he could have been.

So the lead man,
With the plan,
Realized quite soon

How popular it would be
To study
The sad Demise of Louise.

The same system that overcharged
For an assessment
To keep her connected

And educated to a higher degree
Did not connect the dots
That could no longer move

On Scatter Plots
But any conclusion would do
For the study would be read by very few

The pay would make them middle class;
The Pull of feeling elite;
Treating others as if they were living on the street.

Yes that was the way
To raise the ceiling
And it seemed to be so appealing.

A good rant
Would get a large government grant
Much more

Than the cost of the assessment
That could have kept Louise connected.
But the connection was lost

Like a broken telephone
Leaving Louise totally alone
In a world where they refused to hear her speak.

A cyber leak was free to tell the truth
Big Brother said Louise was known,
Though there was no proof to be shown.

EPICS 2: Spy Included

Not even a call to verify
Whether this conclusion
Was just another lie.

Dirty Politics; Shitily managed;
For the evidence was locked
Out of sight.

Behind a door
Nothing new;
Just be glad it didn't happen to you.

And a third world war
Was rumored to be flaming
Across the sea

But no one could see;
What was happening here;
The lack of value was clear;

The cost made them fear
The war that was so far away
Could one day be here.

But not today;
And big brother said
Louise knew who killed her.

But if she really knew him
I know she would have ran away.
I knew it was true

Big Brother was manufacturing consent
Again
As a member of the one percent.

Watch the empty street
So many are gone
Just vanished

They are now half alive behind a wall

Very few
Knew them
At all.

Now Time has gone
World's opportunities closed
To too many;

EPICS 2: Spy Included

While the robo-beast
Surveys
Without a word;

To satisfy the one percent
While manufacturing consent
To be disenfranchised and to be left alone;

Free from pain but never free;
Pushing Louise out of society;
Dirty Politics; Shitily Managed;

In the poorest part of town
No longer designed
For smooth market flow;

Designed as a place
For the Nouveau Poor
To go.

Pretty barriers to channel
Those in cars
To drive past fast.

No longer middle class.

The cop on the beat
Stared at Louise
As if she was living on the street.

No one remembers the day
Before the barriers
Transformed our Right of Way.

Barriers;
To channel the well to do
To drive away.

Barriers;
Called a thing of beauty
Silently doing their duty.

And Big Brother said
He knew them all;
As privacy rights vanished too.

No manual controls;
Just automated;
Water too hot

And water too cold;
Will always be that way
While you grow old.

Chaos;

So the little man can feel like a big man;
He manufactures consent
There is nothing he needs to prevent.

Later; time and evidence would fade;
While big war machines so ready to kill
Were put on parade to give Joe Public a thrill.

Sometimes the wounded are killed
By mistake;
It is hard to know what is made up and fake.

No reason for Big Brother
To repent;
He is part of the one percent.

Little man
Now feels like a big man
After he manufactures consent

One more time again.
He could never win
On a level playing field.

The little man
Lets hate
Control fate

While looking for people all alone;
Their world soon to be turned upside down;
The glass ceiling

Becomes the floor
Just like the way it is done
Many times before.

Oh Beautiful Child
Do not forget who you are;
You are the Son of War.

As Big Brother yanks the chain.
The Demise of Louise
Is hidden under the cover;

Owned by Big Brother.
Just another energy vampire;
Roaming; lost in his pride;

There is nowhere to hide
When you are all alone
Walking in the Negative Zone.

Mean Girls will look so nice
Mean Boys will be as cold as ice.
You; Beautiful Child;

Remember who you are;
You are the Son of War;
Maybe the worst war we have ever had;

Don't feel sad
Don't feel bad
Remember who you are

You are the Son of War.

THE END

SHRUNK

#27. SHRUNK

I

As the world was shrinking
I saw you holding on;
You held on to me too

Without thinking.

Then you brought me down;
I thought I would drown;
In a feeling

That should never be felt on the floor.
The links were so tight
It hurt more than ever before

That night; shrinking value
While some hide in space;
Shrinking privacy;

All over the place
While the Watchers
Stood on corners in the divided city;

One side was pretty
And the other side had
Dead end streets galore;

The Watchers craved blood and nothing more.
Traffic moved too fast
Until it stopped at its regular choking point.

There was just too much smoke
From the fire
And not enough water to put it out.

The Watchers were standing about;
Obsessed with their standing power,
They did not move.

There were broken lines
Interrupted by a shout;
Broken lines;

So many wanted out;
But the Watchers were standing about,
Standing over broken lines,

That could not sustain life;

Observations fading
Never to be seen again
In the same way.

II

Alienation;
Social Degradation;
Lack of entry point

For integration.
Alienation;
Isolation.

The Watchers
Did not share the same values
With the watched.

Alienation;
A hurt sensation
Behind the Red Line.

III

Who could she have been,
If there were less people blocking,
When opportunities were knocking?

He took his ring off
And hid it
In his pocket.

That way
He could take what he could;
And still demand more.

In the Negative Zone
Alienation
Kept most

Behind the Red Line
While the Watchers
Obsessed with their standing power

Remained standing,
Steely faced,
At their post.

EPICS 2: Spy Included

The bravest from the Negative Zone
Dared to roam
Around the pretty side of town

Before the glare grew too hot to handle.

Then the bravest
Were not brave any more
They went back home

And hid behind their door;
For evermore.
The Red Line

Grew to be their comfort zone;
Where they now belonged;
Where they could be left alone;

Slowly dying within;
This alienation
Was the third sin.

While the Watchers stood;

All in a row
On a skid;
The youth just hid;

Forgetting about tomorrow.

IV

The Watchers were standing at every door;
So obsessed with their power while standing,
They did nothing more;

While the fire raged;
The Watchers saw nothing at all;
Drank into the night

As they did many times before.
They looked in the mirror
Before they left the Fancy Inn.

They felt pride for they were so well-dressed;

EPICS 2: Spy Included

They tumbled with the dispossessed,
Leaving them in their aftermath;
Made the Watchers laugh.

The Timocracy had just begun;
The Watchers made the dispossessed run;
While they remained

Obsessed with standing
Door to door.
Not knowing that this was their first sin;

Violating relationships between neighbors.
Acted as they were from above;
Forgot about brotherly love.

The Watchers were standing about
On the pretty side of town;
Without planning time to reflect.

Riches were not maintained,
As they were all standing about;
Watching those from the poor side of town.

Walking about.
Timocracy;
Descendants of an aristocracy;

Now nothing more
Than a bumbling
Bureaucracy.

Riches suffered from neglect,
While the Watchers drank
The public's money away.

The Watchers didn't know any other way;
All they did
Was watch their day fade away

Into a new night

Again; the Watchers ran out of the door
Leaving the Fancy Inn behind
One more time again.

The ghetto was soon in plain view;
That is how they picked Rose;
And kicked her down

EPICS 2: Spy Included

Past the Red Line on the other side of town.

But Rose had died before;
Beside me
On the floor;

So Rose arose; not really living;
Not yet ready to die;
She was in such pain; it made me cry.

Rose was blamed for her failure;
The Watchers success;
They could afford to be well dressed;

Though they never thought of anything new
To do
Or say;

They were Watchers everyday

Standing around watching
As the time went by;
They jumped to conclusions;

But never found solutions.

The Watchers' staring oppressed
And froze many into fear;
Soon many became dispossessed;

More money went out
While the Watchers were standing about
And the producers were too few

To bring money in;
The Watchers watched
While many were liquidated

Even those who were well to do
And not even hated
The cost of living had inflated

The cost to live was now understated.

And Big Brother yelled out his order
To close the border;
For the only growth industry

Pretty city had
Was Fear of Disorder;
And nothing more.

EPICS 2: Spy Included

The fence went up;
The cup
Was now half empty

There was less cause for envy.

Big Brother said he knew what was best;
Bulldozed what he called slums;
Classified the residents bums.

And on the other side
Of the street; past the lights
The people there were called citizens;

And they were so well dressed

Would fight all night
With the dispossessed.
So they could fill up their cup;

"Put your wall up,"
Another Big Brother said.
"And keep it up

So those outsiders can't get in."
As Jealousy became the second sin;
They said all they wanted to do was win;

Still haunted by their first sin.
They pray to the eye in sky
That had broken down.

It was just a machine

Needed an artificial source
Of fuel to move; it needed artificial energy
To groove.

The eye in the sky
Was Big Brother's
Recorder.

Situated
High above;
So Big Brother could watch the border;

The only growth industry
Was Fear
Of Disorder;

Dividing our world so alive;

EPICS 2: Spy Included

We did what we did to survive;
While Electricity was flashing
Above our world of organic matter;

So fragile
And so easy
To tatter.

In a world that was made for life
The Watchers hid in the shadows
Complaining about what they saw

On the other side of the lights;
After a few beers
The Watchers would let loose

All their fears
Into the Negative Zone
Where the poorest of the poor were walking alone.

The city was divided
In two
By Force; same Power

That divided the Earth from the sky and sea;
Sky that seemed to go on
For eternity;

The Nouveau Colony;

Where mysteries were abounding;
The beauty was astounding.
Silently; hearts were pounding;

In these times of war.

Earth's greatest wealth
Was in her people
Made from True Love

Standing in line for bread;
Slept on the street;
They had no bed.

Yes this was the time;
For the Timocrats to rule;
It was a system that was very cruel;

EPICS 2: Spy Included

Designed by the simple minded;
Hate
Was their bait;

Hate opened Hell's gate;
And it was rumored that the Zombie race
Had taken over;

Fear and Hate
Closed minds;
Hate was now in control of Fate.

Timocrats made problems
That they could never resolve;
Timocrats allowed decency to dissolve

We were waiting until the Timocrats could evolve?
The only growth industry
Was the Fear of Disorder.

While the Watchers
Grew more obsessed
With standing at every door.

Waiting for Zombies
To come out
Of the floor.

While the Zombie economy
Dominated
More than ever before.

To us it felt like a police state
Without due process needed
The Watchers would oppress while they greeted

Us; for the only growth industry left
Was the Fear of Disorder
And nothing more.

Many in the Negative Zone
Struggled to stay afloat;
While the Watchers looked remote and stared

At the dispossessed while taking note;
Waiting for another vote;
All they knew was learned by rote;

As they stood on the Pretty Side of the street;

EPICS 2: Spy Included

Those who owned the land
Were the only ones
To give command

So they
Made it forbidden;
For those from the poor side of town

To be seen
On the pretty side of town.
They were called eye sores

For evermore.

The Watchers made it so;
Followed those
They did not know, including Rose.

They turned around so quick
It made Rose feel sick;
Now they accused Rose

Of following them.

The Watchers needed Rose to fit
Their billing code
So they could get paid

While channeling
Tax money from the poorest part of town
To make the other side of town

Even more pretty;
While they sent Rose to the Shrink
Hired by the Watchers' boss;

Who wrote in Rose's new file with red ink;

Dissolved her identity;
She could no longer be
Who she used to be;

She couldn't even think.

Rose changed, almost over night
And would never be free.
She was now too broken inside

Victim of the self-fulfilling prophecy;

And labelled for life
While the Watchers looked at Rose
As if she were a Zombie coming out of the floor.

EPICS 2: Spy Included

Rose wilted
And faded away
To become nothing more.

The Watchers now watched Rose's every move
So they could build a case against her
Fitting her into their billing code.

Her sense of worth
Would be diminished
For evermore.

Rose would lose her sense of self;
Transferred into Watchers' wealth;
She was now shrunk;

Often put into cells

Of solitary;
The gain for the Watchers was purely monetary.
As she screamed out in Psychic Pain

No one came;
No one knew her at all;
For Rose there was no gain.

Alienation;
A hurt sensation
Haunting the Timocrat Nation.

It was just another day;
The Watchers were authorized
To watch Rose every day;

The pain for Rose
Never went away;
Living under this new way;

For the only growth industry
In the Pretty City
Was fear of Social Disorder;

And Rose was too young to hide her heart.

Alienation;
The Watchers win;
Power corrupts the soul;

This was the fourth sin.

The Watchers classified
Rose to be insane
As they watched her rolling

In Psychic Pain.
The Watchers picked Rose
To use in their social experiment;

Rose's pain hung from her Psyche;
Felt like cement;
Rose's pain brought her down;

It hurt so bad;
She would rather drown
In Eternity where she could be free

For evermore.

No; it was too soon
To let go; Rose could not fade away;
The Watchers told Rose to repent

And to bow down to the One Percent.

The Watchers watched
While taking notes;
Now Rose would never be the same again.

The Watchers were pleased
With the work they had done.
Now they could shun

Rose; speaking about her
But never to her;
For evermore.

Rose was now processed into the Billing Code;
The Watchers self-prophesied;
One day Rose would explode.

V

Success was measured in Quantity;
Not in Quality.
The Watchers knew who voted for who;

Sometimes names were put on a list;
If they did not vote
For the well to do.

EPICS 2: Spy Included

Fear ruled; while the able were able to flee;
The empty spaces
Gave new opportunity

For the Timocrat Nation
So many lost in Alienation;
Still found Love

To be the best sensation;
Able to lift them beyond
The Red Line on the ground;

Love helped them fly
To new heights;
Never reached before;

When stuck behind
The Red Line
Dividing Pretty City

Part of Timocrat Nation;

Only growth industry
Was the Fear of Disorder;
Gave the Watchers so much opportunity

To watch
Without ever
Having to see.

VI

The police were militarized;
They pierced the youth
With their eyes.

Timocrats wasted youth's time
While they were being paid
By the hour;

The Watchers
Forced youth
To explain their presence

Everyday
Until they either ran away
Or stayed hidden behind the red line.

VII

Pete
Loved Rose
And came to visit

When he was allowed.
Pete too was lost in the crowd
Behind the Red Line.

Sometimes
Pete
Would share

The little he had to eat.

One day
Pete saw Rose
Hooked up

To a machine without a heart;
Soon the frustration
Tore them apart.

VIII

Lies needed no evidence.
For there was no evidence
To give.

Names were listed so casually;
As people not yet dispossessed
Begged for privacy;

We were all told to shop locally
But when we left
The part of town

Behind the Red Line
We felt put down
As the micro-managers

Asked for our life story
Before they let us
In their door

That was watched by Watchers
More intensely
Than ever before.

We felt degraded;
The hurt lingered
For evermore.

Watchers took notes
As they stood by the door
Steely faced;

They never spoke;
They grunted
While counting votes;

As the ragged people
Returned books to the library.
They were watched by the police gone military

No longer civil in their duty; they shouted the order
For the only growth industry
Was Fear of Disorder.

IX

Tell me why
Some get ahead
While putting others down?

Tell me why.

X

Hear the Fear
Of Public Disorder
The only growth industry

In the town; was fenced in by a wall;
The xenophobes controlled it all;
Outsiders were not welcomed anymore;

The town was toxic;
The youth felt sick
With fear.

For the militarized police were always near.

Youth needed love to grow
But the atmosphere of Fear
Kept them stunted;

Fear had taken hold;
Many felt hunted;
A strip mall replaced the community hall;

EPICS 2: Spy Included

Where everything of value was sold
Before it turned to rust
And faded away.

While the old feared the young
Big Brothers' rule
Had just begun.

It stayed that way
Until the Youth
Grew Old.

Big Brother did not speak;
And everything you said would be used
Against you the following week.

This was how the Watchers got ahead;
Even though such a Timocracy
Was costly; some also said

A travesty of justice;
For Fear
Grew in the collective head.

The able were able to flee;
Spaces of opportunity were now free;
For the Watchers who were only able

To watch and take notes;
Demanded votes;
Learned by reciting rotes.

The young; the ones not missing;
Stopped believing in Love;
So they were never get caught kissing

Under the apple tree
Of Forbidden Knowledge;
They had lost their courage.

The Timocrats
Worshiped their mechanical eye in the sky
While never doubting the rules

Of their Timocratic world.

THE END

BROKEN CHAIN

#28. BROKEN CHAIN

I

In Ghetto Town
Everyone is standing around
Putting each other down.

The chain
Reaction;
Never ending

In satisfaction;

Alienation;
A hurt sensation;
Imprisoned by a generation

Without imagination;
Lost in a war;
Bad memories awake

When the broken hearted sleep;
So lost in the Negative Zone;
Losing their imagination

Was their first mistake.

EPICS 2: Spy Included

They take what they can
As they bulldoze the rest;
Leaving many dispossessed.

In the Ghetto Town
Wearing a cross; wearing a frown;
Mean girls putting poor boys down.

"What isn't being replaced by a global,
Live and let die Economy?
Poor Boy asked to know one in particular;

Things were changing and were not so familiar;
Scaled; interconnected; global;
Sometimes silently;

Sometimes vocal;

Watchers stare;
They don't care;
They wave to the Mean Girls

Who are dressed for success.
They can't connect substantially
As they grow old locally;

And so divided.

Downtown Streets
Growing into speedways;
Hostile to walkers and bikers.

Global impact;
A fact of life
That doesn't change;

Mean Girls
So vain and protected;
Never loved for themselves

Barbie Dolls
Sitting on shelves.
How they laugh

During the Mind War;
The war with no end
The mind; Infinite Space;

Without curiosity
Lost capacity
Generation without imagination;

Or anything;

Poor Boy has no place;
And how they laugh
While he is displaced;

Mean Girls carry their fear card;
In their tight blue jeans;
They catch poor boy off guard;

As they stress their targets out;
With accusations
Hear them shout;

"There is only one way out."

No defence; their eyes are everywhere;
They are watching;
Those ghettoized on the other side;

Social Disorder
Growth Industry
So the watchers can buy bling;

Off the street;
Across the sea;
Politics of Vanity;

How they watch but cannot see.
The growing gap
In a live and die economy.

How they watch and cannot see
The dispossessed and neglected;
Displaced and unprotected.

How they watch but cannot see;
As they exclude and collude
Destroying Poor Boy's will to live

"Only one way out"
They shout;
You will never fit

Into this closed knit
Society;
"Only one way out

Or die in anxiety."

The weapons of choice;
Worn Porn;
Destroys assumption of innocence;

Destroys common sense;
Social Order
Right side and wrong side

Of the Tracks
Behind the red line
Ghost suppliers

From who knows where
Secret Police dressed to kill
Dressed to thrill.

Sometimes like a mean girl
Who has never been loved for her self
Barbie Doll on a shelf

Poor boy willing to give love a try;
Born on the poor side of town;
Too young to give up and die;

The militarized police
Already know his face
Telling him to know his place;

City planning with class assumptions;
Social Disorder
As barriers on the dark side of town

Destroy civility somehow
Nowhere to cross
Accept under the bridge

Where the desperate are displaced;
The Mean Girls shout;
"There is only way out".

Mean Girls have never been loved
Just for themselves;
Barbie dolls sitting on shelves.

Poor Boy's

Ancestors were born in the Negative Zone too;
They too were excluded
While the cronies colluded.

EPICS 2: Spy Included

Detained in concrete
As the Watchers wave
To the Mean Girls

Old money;
In bred style to
Impoverish those

If they don't go;
Pace is slow;
Small Town Culture

In a Big Box City;
Brutality
Is second nature

While toy guns
Are waved around
For fun

As the mean boys
From the pretty part of town
Run Poor Boys down;

On the other side of the lights;
Rich Boys pick fights;
To fill the boring nights;

While they deaden their souls;
Loss of imagination
Lost in alienation

A hurt sensation

Standing on the other side of the street.
Poor Boys are under suspicion
Micromanaged to death

By cruel fools
Who don't follow their own rules;
The only growth industry

Is the fear of disorder
Everyone just feels sadder
Inside they feel madder;

EPICS 2: Spy Included

While downtown streets
Grow into speedways;
The community hall

Is now a mall.
Mean Girls
Left church early

Looking so girly
With hair unnaturally curly;
They wave to the Watchers so burly.

Mean Girls strut
Then cross the street
To look for action and satisfaction;

II

The Watchers point out
Poor Boy without a cent.
Mean Girls get ready

To torment
And to manufacture consent.
Mean Girls are never loved for themselves;

Just Barbie Dolls sitting on shelves.

The Watchers shout,
"We are the new global order,
Our authority knows no border.

We want all Poor Boys
Out of sight;
For this is Sunday night

And the mighty dollar
Has holy power
For those who pray for it everyday;

If you have none go away."
Poor Boy heard
The harsh words;

Brought on feelings of alienation
Medicalized
As a pathology without an apology;

Or common sense.

EPICS 2: Spy Included

For money had "in God we trust"
Written all over it
While it jingles

In the Watchers' pockets.
While the Mean Girls
Strut their stuff;

Had their noses up in the air;
Few could care
For the Mean Girls;
Even though their hearts raged;

Poor boys were being watched and processed
By the Militarized Police State;
With a pretty boy as its head;

Industry of alienation
A hurt sensation
For the indebted generation

Without imagination.

Indebted to old men
Getting ready to die
Going back to their home in the sky.

III

And on the fringe of Ghetto Town
Deer
Were still free; before they were shot.

They had no fear;
Even though
The Machine State was growing

While feeding from
Contracted funds
To Watch but never know

Those herded into skid row.

As affordable housing
Was bulldozed down
The militarized Watchers

EPICS 2: Spy Included

Watched everyone in town;
Accept those in their clique;
There were allowed in the circle;

Allowed to speak.

The Watchers waved to the Mean Girls
Across the street
Who were kicking Poor Boy down;

He was from the poorest part of town;
The Mean Girls said
He filled us with fear

We would sue him if he had a penny to his name
But we will hurt him all the same
Poor Boy is the only one to blame;

So easy to forget his name.
He will wish he was never born;
Thanks to our weaponized porn.

Money linked
Those who had it
To the chain;

And there was nothing much more
Left to link us together
Nothing much to gain but pain.

Barriers and round-abouts were placed

In the streets
To channel traffic
To the mall;

And on the fringe
Wild Life
Lived

But there was no plan
To curb market forces
Accept in our part of town.

EPICS 2: Spy Included

Barriers blocked access;
Legislated poverty;
Property in distress

In our upside down world.

Mean Girls and Watchers drove way too fast
Too dangerous to turn;
So they say;

Members from the coalition
Always get their way
Backing into traffic everyday;

Members of group think
Spin you around
In their loop;

Small town on a Sunday night;
Mean Girls kicking Poor Boys down
While growing old way too fast.

Mean Girls never loved for themselves
Still doing it
In a car parked in the underpass.

Hate feeds
Alienation
From each other

Stress feeds
Alienation
From themselves.

As their teeth rot
Their belly grows
And they don't even notice;

Until it is too late
To change fate
While they call those

On the other side
Of the lights
Trash

Just because they have less cash
For they had been excluded
While the cronies colluded.

A long time ago; alienation;

Now the glass ceiling
Has become the floor
As we are all pushed through the revolving door

Once more.

Legislated poverty
Was never called by name
Neither was God.

IV

We all knew the impact just the same.
As the dead end street;
Were numbered; they had no name.

Surrounded by parking lots
Encroached
On Nature's beauty.

Lost sense of civic duty.

Not planned for public good;
Devaluing property
Into a slum;

Treating us as if we were bums;
No longer Equity Tenants;
Assets

Are now toxic.
In the Negative Zone;
Thought you could never feel so alone.

No repair for this Urban Sprawl
One day it will be bulldozed
To make a playground

EPICS 2: Spy Included

For the rich;
The wild life living on the fringe
Could only watch

While the Mean Girls
Feared those
They persecuted.

The unemployed
Were treated rough
And the hypocrisy caused feelings of rage.

The police state without connectors
Paved Paradise
The way we had been warned.

There was nowhere for children to play

Or for Nature to do her stuff;

V
Broken Chain
Man against Man
To control Means of Production;

Surplus from Production
Outcome of Production
Is no longer true

I saw how machines
Replaced you
Without a tear

Without a fear

EPICS 2: Spy Included

While the Mean Girls
Standing at the front door
At the Local Dive

While their own worn porn
Destroyed love
For love was not that tough.

Accused you
Of being destitute
No tenderness at all.

Cultural Decline;
Very few
Knew their own minds.

Group think
Excluded those on the other side of the tracks
While the cronies colluded

In plain sight
On Sunday night
Everyone was uptight.

As the Mean Girls
Picked a fight with Poor Boy,
Made Poor Boy feel hopeless;

Overnight;
And it was mostly the hypocrisy
That caused his heart to rage;

As he hung from the ceiling
He wondered why the world
Had lost all the good feeling

He felt as a boy;
Always a Poor Boys
But could still feel joy.

For he had the soul of a poet;
He saw beauty
Where others could not;

And he felt pain
When others would not;
And perhaps same soul

Will fly
Into another Poor Boy
Too angry to die.

While the Mean Girls
Complained all day long
About those closest to them;

That were still living;
It was Sunday night
And the chain was broken;

Their pain had awoken;

Mean girls want to leave town
For a better life
But don't know how;

They were too afraid
Of progress
And only those that left

Soon came back
To the small town
Where their ancestors were born

Now feeling so worn;
They understood
How the town had regressed.

In all the spin
Many closed their eyes to survive
In the ‘live and let die’ global economy.

What had been lost;
Collective Consciousness
Excluded those on the other side of the lights.

Only the birds in the sky were free;

Mean Girls; rigid and blue;
Prejudice made them as cold as ice;
When they touched you.

It didn't feel nice.
Concluding and colluding
Fed their fear; the price;

Stayed with their own kind
They never knew their own mind;
Fought with those excluded.

Mean Girls; the Gate Keepers;
Laughed at the broken hearted.
The chosen few were certain to win.

For everyone knew

Manufacturing war-stuff
Was more profitable
Than filling the world with love.

THE END

Produced by S.E. McKenzie Productions
First Print Edition October 2015

Enquiries: 1(778)992-2453
Mailing Address:
S. E. McKenzie Productions
168 B 5th St.
Courtenay, BC
V9N 1J4

Email Address:
messidartha@aol.com

http://www.amazon.com/SarahMcKenzie/e/B00H9RWX48/

www.ingramcontent.com/pod-product-compliance
Lightning Source LLC
LaVergne TN
LVHW020925090426
835512LV00020B/3205